FREE
FOR ALL
COOKING

Also by Jules E. Dowler Shepard

The First Year: Celiac Disease and Living Gluten-Free

Nearly Normal Cooking for Gluten-Free Eating

FREE
FOR ALL
COOKING

150 EASY GLUTEN-FREE, ALLERGY-FRIENDLY RECIPES THE WHOLE FAMILY CAN ENJOY

Jules E. Dowler Shepard

Da Capo
LIFE
LONG

A Member of the Perseus Books Group

Many of the designations used by manufacturers and sellers to distinguish their products are claimed as trademarks. Where those designations appear in this book and Da Capo Press was aware of a trademark claim, the designations have been printed in initial capital letters.

Design and production by Trish Wilkinson
Set in 11 point Minion

Library of Congress Cataloging-in-Publication Data

Shepard, Jules E. Dowler.
    Free for all cooking : 150 easy gluten-free, allergy-friendly recipes the whole family can enjoy / Jules E. Dowler Shepard.—1st Da Capo Press ed.
        p.   cm.
Includes index.
    ISBN 978-0-7382-1395-8 (pbk. : alk. paper) 1. Gluten-free diet—Recipes. 2. Celiac disease—Diet therapy. I. Title.
RM237.86.S54 2010
641.5'638—dc22   2010029917

Published by Da Capo Press
A Member of the Perseus Books Group
www.dacapopress.com

Note: The information in this book is true and complete to the best of our knowledge. This book is intended only as an informative guide for those wishing to know more about health issues. In no way is this book intended to replace, countermand, or conflict with the advice given to you by your own physician. The ultimate decision concerning care should be made between you and your doctor. We strongly recommend you follow his or her advice. Information in this book is general and is offered with no guarantees on the part of the authors or Da Capo Press. The authors and publisher disclaim all liability in connection with the use of this book.

Da Capo Press books are available at special discounts for bulk purchases in the U.S. by corporations, institutions, and other organizations. For more information, please contact the Special Markets Department at the Perseus Books Group, 2300 Chestnut Street, Suite 200, Philadelphia, PA, 19103, or call (800) 810-4145, ext. 5000, or e-mail special.markets @perseusbooks.com.

To the patient women of my family. My great-grandmother, my two grandmothers, and my mother each shared with me their recipes, baking secrets, and always at least a pinch of joy in the kitchen—these gifts have found their way into everything I now so happily share with others.

Contents

PART I

❋ Essentials of Gluten-Free Cooking

PART II

The Recipes

CHAPTER 3 ✳ BREADS AND ROLLS   99

CHAPTER 3 ✽ BREADS AND ROLLS *continued*

CHAPTER 4 ✽ SOUPS   129

CHAPTER 5 ✽ MAIN EVENTS   139

CHAPTER 6 ❋ DESSERTS   169

CHAPTER 6 ❋ DESSERTS *continued*

Acknowledgments

This book has been in the making for many years. Before my last cookbook was even published in 2006, I had embarked upon my free newsletter, in which I publish a new recipe each week for all my readers to enjoy. This regimine meant that I have had to create a new recipe each week as well, thus setting me on course for another cookbook within a few short years. During that time, however, I also began teaching cooking classes and traveling around the country, speaking as an expert in gluten-free cooking and living. I wrote another book, *The First Year: Celiac Disease and Living Gluten-Free*, and founded a gluten-free flour company—Jules Gluten Free. Not only did these other activities keep me quite busy, they taught me a lot more about our gluten-free community.

Folks coming to the gluten-free table come for many different reasons, but most have been on a long journey to discover the key to improving their health. Along the way, many, if not most, learn that they have other food intolerances as well. Be they allergies or intolerances, as with gluten, if your body doesn't like a particular food, it needs to come out of your diet. That reality is harder for some than for others, and certainly harder with certain ingredients than with others. Many families are contending with multiple and differing food restrictions. Helping these folks in my classes, lectures, and consultations, as well as through my newsletter and e-mails, I came to know that my next book needed to help people do more than just understand how to successfully remove gluten from their diets.

So, I must first express how grateful I am to all those along the way who have shared their food needs and restrictions with me; their experiences and the solutions I have crafted for them inspired much of the content of this book. To the loyal readers of my other books and of my weekly newsletter, I value all the feedback you give me. *Free for All Cooking* represents a compilation of many reader-requested recipes and favorites throughout the years of my newsletter.

No labor of love is ever possible without support, and for that constant encouragement, assistance, and understanding, I must thank my wonderful friends and family. Among this battery of supporters were taste-testers, bakers, and honest critics of my recipes, as well as others who entertained my kids as I worked to meet deadlines. These dear friends are the only reasons this book was ever finished on time! Mary, Monique, Danielle, Brooke, Kathy, Gabrielle, Trish, Laurie, Sandi, Kathy, Nina, and Haley allowed me to work without (too much) guilt that I wasn't spending every moment with my children, whom I knew were always having fun with my friends and their kids! If my parents lived closer, they would have been ever-present recipe tasters and child tenders; however, distance could not dim their constant encouragement and love, which has always buoyed me. Such unconditional love has carried me not just through this project, but over other hurdles in my life as well.

Two other people deserve special credit for making this book everything I had hoped. Kathy Witte was instrumental in the beginning stages of this book's creation, by not only helping give it the organization it so needed, but also by reading every recipe to be sure that they were clear and simple enough for even first-time bakers to follow. Her counsel was always blunt, and always right! She made this book better for her contributions, and I so appreciate her for it! Jeff Rasmussen worked tirelessly—always with a smile—and never complained about the odd times of day I would create a new recipe and need a professional food photograph. He spent hours upon hours, often waiting for just the right natural light to come streaming through the window, so that he could get the *real food* shots I wanted (stock food photos are a pet peeve of mine!). His eye and patient angling brought light to such minute crumbs that it helped me to focus on more than the big picture and challenged me to create even more delicate and delectable dishes. Traces of his cheeriness, creativity, support, critiques, laughter, and love have made their way into every part of this book, as they have in my life, and I will be forever grateful.

Dr. Alessio Fasano and his team at the University of Maryland Center for Celiac Research, in particular Pam King and Pam Cureton, have once again provided invaluable support and information to me in my work. And once again, Dr. Fasano has taken time out of his inhumanly busy schedule to grace the pages of my third book.

What's more, he continues to make invaluable contributions with his pioneering work in the celiac community; his dedication to preventing, understanding, and mitigating celiac disease is a light for everyone living with CD. He also has supported and encouraged me professionally, and our friendship has been a bright spot on my own celiac journey.

An author can never say enough about their agent, and it certainly holds true for me as well. Marilyn Allen knows the crucial role she has played in bringing to life this, my third book. I only wish she lived closer, so she could sample all my bake-outs!

Finally, I am so appreciative of the efforts of my editor, Katie McHugh, in promoting this book and its vision. The team at DaCapo Press has embraced my vision of teaching readers how to fashion each recipe to suit their own family's dietary needs, substituting only where necessary. This result is key to ensuring that these recipes are truly delicious and safe for each reader's particular food restriction without compromising on taste.

To you all, a heartfelt thanks!

Foreword

BY ALESSIO FASANO, MD

Medical Director, The University of Maryland Center for Celiac Research

Everyone working in the field of nutrition is well aware that we are in the midst of a food intolerance epidemic—the number of people suffering from a variety of reactions to specific foods increases daily. While the specific reason for this surge is unknown, the incredibly fast pace with which this phenomenon is spreading through the population suggests a strong correlation with a change in our environment. Regardless of the cause, the result is that more and more people are forced to eliminate specific components from their diet, affecting one of the most enjoyable activities in our lives: eating good food.

Celiac disease (CD) is perhaps the best-known example of this phenomenon. CD, or gluten sensitive enteropathy, is an immune mediated chronic condition targeting the intestines, rendering them incapable of properly handling certain foods. This, in turn, leads to a wide range of clinical manifestations of variable severity. In addition to the typical malabsorption symptoms (e.g., chronic diarrhea, weight loss, abdominal distension), CD can manifest itself in symptoms that can affect any of the body's organ systems. Because CD is now more widely recognized, a smaller proportion of patients actually present with gastrointestinal symptoms typical of CD. Today, non-intestinal symptoms are more prominent, including anemia, joint pain, chronic fatigue, short stature, skin lesions, and neurological and behavioral problems (including peripheral neuropathy, epilepsy, dementia, schizophrenia, and seizure with intracranial calcifications). Because CD often presents in an atypical or even "silent" manner, the vast majority of cases still go undiagnosed. Such cases carry the risk of long-term complications in adolescence and adulthood, including osteoporosis, infertility, miscarriages, cancer, or the onset of other autoimmune diseases.

To further complicate matters, CD is not the only way you can react to gluten. There is now a recently identified condition called gluten sensitivity that affects many more people than CD. The bright side is that, even though it can often clinically mimic CD, gluten sensitivity is not an autoimmune disease like CD, and therefore does not destroy the intestine. Nevertheless, people affected by gluten sensitivity also need to avoid gluten to regain their state of health.

Until recently, the geographical distribution of CD and gluten sensitivity was mostly restricted to Europe. New epidemiological studies indicate that these conditions are common in other industrialized countries, such as the United States, Canada, and Australia as well as in many developing countries, suggesting that the "global village of CD and gluten sensitivity" has a worldwide distribution. It appears that no continent on the planet is spared by the disease. It is projected that approximately 3 million Americans could be affected by CD and approximately 20 million suffer with gluten sensitivity, both with only a fraction actually diagnosed.

The trigger for CD and gluten sensitivity involves grains like wheat, rye, and barley, which contain a protein called gluten that initiates the body's damaging, defensive response. Luckily, there is an outright cure for both of these conditions: adhering to a strict gluten-free diet—an endeavor made all the more difficult by three related issues.

The first, gluten's nearly pervasive presence (and in many countries an unlabeled presence) in many of the foods we eat. While increased awareness of CD and gluten sensitivity has led to an increase in the number and variety of gluten-free products available, mainstream food stores, however, are still playing catch up in carrying many of them, and those that do, because they're still a specialty item, price them as premium products, compared to their gluten-containing counterparts.

The second challenge for those eating gluten-free, and the reasons most often responsible for failure to adhere to the diet, is a lack of information, poor awareness among health care professionals, and major confusion around what is safe and what is not. Once patients are diagnosed, it is not unusual that they are advised to go on a gluten-free diet and left to go it alone. One of Jules Shepard's missions in her life has been to provide that sorely missed guidance, expertise, and comfort these bewildered and often daunted people need. Her second book, *The First Year: Celiac Disease and Living Gluten Free*, offered step-by-step, week-by-week information and encouragement to the newly diagnosed, having navigated the transition to living gluten-free on her own more than ten years ago.

With this much-needed book, *Free for All Cooking*, Jules now has embraced with her typical passion the third challenge a growing number of people eating gluten-free must overcome: the fact that people with CD often develop other food intolerances, the most frequent being lactose intolerance, further restricting the foods they can safely ingest. Routine activities such as shopping and cooking, combined with new cross-contamination concerns, while also trying to maintain a balanced and palatable diet together can become simply overwhelming for someone eliminating gluten and yet another food or two, *without the creative and sage advice Jules offers in this book*. With her invaluable personal experience and a unique touch of humanity, Jules patiently walks you through the major lifestyle change that CD and gluten sensitivity represent. Having personally had the opportunity to taste some of Jules' recipes, I will admit I was amazed by the fact that you cannot tell the difference from their traditional counterparts. With this valuable book, Jules again proves that eliminating foods from your diet need not cost you taste, variety, nutrition, or require more than basic skill in the kitchen. With the health and happiness of millions at stake, Jules' book plays an important role in our health and of those we love.

Preface

More and more people are altering the way they eat because of food allergies, food sensitivities, or other health concerns such as celiac disease, diabetes, Crohn's Disease, IBS, or a host of others. Odds are that you, a family member, or someone you know has been affected by one of these conditions and changed their diet accordingly. We're not alone. The numbers of us affected by food restrictions are staggering—more than 12 million Americans—and growing each day.*

Eight foods (milk, eggs, peanuts, tree nuts, wheat, soybeans, fish, and shellfish) account for a full 90 percent of all food-allergic reactions in the United States, and so in 2006, the FDA began requiring food manufacturers to identify these foods when used as ingredients (gluten is still not required to be listed as an ingredient).** Manufacturers are not required to advise consumers on their packaging that a given product is produced in a facility that also produces one of these food allergens, although some manufacturers do abide by this voluntary advisory language. Even today, though, it can still be tricky to find manufactured foods that everyone on your list can enjoy safely. I have counseled families all across the country who are grappling with feeding

---

* More than 12 million Americans have a diagnosed allergy to a particular food, which can include gluten. "Food Allergy Facts and Statistics," Food Allergy & Anaphylaxis Network, retrieved June 27, 2010 from http://www.foodallergy.org/page/facts-and-stats. In addition, an estimated 15–25 percent of American consumers currently report looking for gluten-free products. While 1 percent of the population is estimated to have celiac disease, fully 15 percent is estimated to suffer from "gluten sensitivity."

** Pursuant to the Food Allergen Labeling and Consumer Protection Act of 2004 (FALCPA).

a family whose members have a variety of food restrictions. One family I recall had one child who was allergic to milk, another with gluten sensitivity and lactose intolerance, and still another with egg and nut allergies. Does everyone eat a different meal? How do you find options that are tasty *and* affordable? Many of us with food restrictions are returning to our own kitchens to create safe solutions that also save us time and money. This strategy also provides the opportunity to make fresh, healthy foods that are delicious enough to serve to anyone.

So just how do you change your favorite recipes into ones you can share with your whole family, regardless of their food restrictions, or bring to a dinner party with food-sensitive friends? While there is no magic cure for celiac disease or for food allergies and sensitivities, there are fortunately many delicious ways to avoid the culprits behind these problems—and you'll find these solutions in *Free for All Cooking*.

I hope you enjoy these easy, fulfilling, healthy recipes that can be tailored to your specific dietary restriction(s). As you're about to discover, preparing delicious and nutritious Free for All foods can be simple, creative, nutritious, and fun! Savor the foods you thought you might never again taste and prepare them for your whole family to enjoy together.

To your health,
jules

PART I

Essentials of Gluten-Free Cooking

Ingredients and Substitutions

BASIC, NATURALLY GLUTEN-FREE FOODS

This list of examples is by no means comprehensive, but rather demonstrates the range of naturally gluten-free foods that are safe for those with celiac disease or gluten sensitivity when prepared without gluten-containing ingredients.

Butter	Honey
Cheeses (most)	Lentils
Chicken	Meats
Eggs	Milk
Fish	Nuts
Fresh Fruit and 100% Fruit Juices	Seeds
Fresh Vegetables and 100% Vegetable Juices	Shellfish
	Sugar
Grits	

SAFE, GLUTEN-FREE INGREDIENTS
(GRAINS, PSEUDOCEREALS, BEANS, AND MORE)

These products are safe in any form, so long as they are not mixed with other non-gluten-free foods or produced in an environment risking cross-contamination with gluten-containing foods.

Agar agar	Oats (certified gluten-free)
Amaranth	Pea flour
Arrowroot Powder	Potatoes, potato starch, potato flour
Buckwheat	Rice and rice flour
Cabernet flour	Sago starch/pearls
Chia seeds/flour	Seeds (like sesame, poppy, sunflower)
Corn (maize)	
Flax seeds and flaxseed meal	Sorghum flour
Legumes/beans and flours (e.g., fava, garbanzo, garfava)	Soy and soy flour
	Tapioca (cassava, manioc) starch and flour
Lentils and lentil flour	Teff
Millet flour	Quinoa and quinoa flour
Montina flour	Wild rice
Nut flours	

NON-GLUTEN-FREE GRAINS AND
OTHER INGREDIENTS TO AVOID

These products are not considered gluten-free in any form or amount.

Bread or bread products containing wheat flour—like breading, coating mixes, or *panko*	Couscous
	Durum
	Einkorn
Barley	Emmer
Barley malt	Farina
Bulgur	Farro

continues

Graham flour

Kamut

Kashi

Malt (unless from corn)

Matzo/matzah

Modified food starch made
    from Wheat*

Orzo

Rye

Seitan

Semolina

Spelt

Triticale

Wheat

INGREDIENTS:
A HANDY SUBSTITUTION GUIDE

Like anything else, when it comes to allergy-free cooking, necessity is truly the mother of invention. If you are inclined at all to experiment as you cook and bake, you will inevitably find your own substitutions with time. But if you need a solution immediately (who doesn't, right?), then give these proven replacements a try. These tips and substitution recipes should help you transform other traditional recipes to allergy-friendly ones to suit your needs. Follow the guide as well when choosing substitutions throughout my recipes; make notes and remember which ones work best for you in which recipes, so you can return to them again with confidence.

Flour

All-purpose wheat flour is what everyone in Western cultures has been accustomed to eating and using in baking. It is ubiquitous in every grocery store as a stand-alone product or as an ingredient in almost any prepackaged baking mix. However, for those with celiac disease or gluten sensitivity, it must be avoided at all costs.

Wheat flour contains gluten—a protein that gives a batter and dough elasticity to hold together, form air bubbles, rise, and have a moist crumb. The good news is that there are many gluten-free flours available; the problem is that none will stand on its

---

* In the United States, "modified food starch" or "starch" refers to starches derived from corn or potatoes. Starches derived from other grains like wheat must be noted on the food label. "Following a Gluten-Free Diet," Beth Israel Deaconess Medical Center (January 2006).

own as an adequate replacement for wheat flour. Typically, a blend of multiple gluten-free flours is needed to achieve a good baking result. In addition, gluten-free recipes must generally include xanthan gum or guar gum—two products that can largely replace gluten's elasticity.

Until recently, most gluten-free foods failed to satisfy all these requirements, thus earning quite a bad taste reputation. However, gluten-free food need no longer disappoint! Still, if you're new to the world of gluten-free, it's easy to be overwhelmed by the dozens of gluten-free flours available, and easy to be confused while trying to find a flour mixture that could adequately substitute for regular wheat flour (I wrote an entire chapter on these flours in my last book, *The First Year: Celiac Disease and Living Gluten Free*)! For simplicity's sake, I will focus here on only the flour combinations that best mimic all-purpose wheat flour, so that you can most easily, economically, and successfully make traditional wheat flour recipes, gluten-free.

Many of the recipes in this cookbook call for my patent-pending blend of gluten- and allergy-free flour (**Jules Gluten Free All Purpose Flour**). This flour is available for purchase, or if you choose to mix your own all-purpose gluten-free flour blend, I've provided a recipe for you on page 8.

I devised this blend for my own use after nearly two years of experimentation as I searched for a gluten-free flour that would perform well in any type of recipe. Tired of having to purchase so many different gluten-free flours and mix them myself for every different recipe, offended at the price of each individual gluten-free flour or gum ingredient, and always disappointed at the results in my gluten-free baked goods, I determined to create my own all-purpose gluten-free flour blend that saved me time, money, and aggravation and, of course, that produced amazing results in every recipe. I now use it exclusively in my cooking and baking and recommend it to all my clients as the simplest, safest, most consistent, and most economical way to prepare delicious gluten- and allergy-free foods for your family.

I hear from folks every day who have emptied their own cabinets of gluten-free flour ingredients in favor of this one mixture, and who swear that it has changed their gluten-free lifestyles as it has changed mine. It's for this reason that I use it in all my baking recipes and why I feel so strongly that it is the best ingredient for you as well.

At first, I mixed the flour for myself in my own kitchen, but I soon learned the hard way that many gluten-free flours are either difficult to find or—incredibly—are not always manufactured in certified gluten-free facilities. So, I began to manufacture my blend through a certified gluten- and allergy-free facility (free of the top eight allergens as listed by the FDA), in order to guarantee for myself and for my customers that the flour is of the highest quality and safety level possible.

You are certainly free to use any other combination of gluten-free flours you choose in place of my blend in these recipes, but if you do so, be sure to also include guar or xanthan gum (already included in my Jules Gluten Free All Purpose Flour) in the correct proportions (approximately 1 teaspoon gum to every cup of flour) to ensure proper binding so that your recipes do not crumble and fall apart. Also, because an alternative flour blend may have different properties, your results may vary.

Premixed Flour Blends

All-purpose gluten-free flour blends are available premixed, but buyer beware. If the mix you select does not already contain xanthan or guar gum, you must also purchase that expensive ingredient and determine the correct proportion to add to your recipe. One teaspoon of xanthan or guar gum for every total cup of gluten-free flour will generally work well in most recipes.

In addition, some of these mixtures perform better than others. Some include flours derived from beans (guar, fava, etc.) which have an aftertaste that may not appeal to all palates or in all dishes. Mixtures heavy in rice flour will tend to be gritty and still others utilizing potato flour (not potato starch) often require doubling the liquids in a given recipe due to this particular flour's drying effects.

If you find that using a particular gluten-free flour blend produces less airy results than you expect, or your baked goods do not rise as much as you would like, try increasing the amount of gluten-free baking powder in your recipe and/or lowering your oven temperature and cooking longer. Cooking on the convection setting (not all ovens have this feature) at a temperature 25 degrees lower than the static oven temperature called for by your recipe will also often help to increase the rise in your recipe.

Make Your Own Gluten-Free Flour Blend

The recipes in this book call for an all-purpose gluten-free flour blend with a starch-to-bulk-flour ratio that helps keep recipes from being too heavy or dense. I find that it makes life so much easier to be able to rely on one go-to, truly all-purpose flour for every kind of recipe—just like in my pre-gluten-free baking days—so I rely on one flour blend for nearly all my cooking and baking.

With that in mind, here is my base recipe using readily available ingredients you can mix yourself to create your own gluten-free flour blend. (I have listed alternative grains in parentheses, in the event you cannot tolerate certain ingredients in this base blend, or if you prefer a more whole-grain taste.) Use this flour as a one-for-one substitution for white wheat flour in traditional recipes, or use in the recipes in this book wherever gluten-free all-purpose flour is named as an ingredient. If you prefer not to shop for and mix your own, **Jules Gluten Free All Purpose Flour** is available online in premixed 5- and 50-pound bags. More information and recipes using the flour may be found on my website, JulesGlutenFree.com.

Jules' Homemade Flour Mix

MAKES 4 CUPS

1 cup arrowroot powder (or tapioca starch)
1 cup potato starch (or tapioca starch or arrowroot powder)
1 cup very fine white rice flour (or sorghum flour or millet flour)
½ cup buckwheat flour (or millet flour, sorghum flour, or brown rice flour)
½ cup tapioca starch (or cornstarch)
4 teaspoons xanthan gum (may be corn-based) or guar gum

▸ Whisk all ingredients together in a large mixing bowl, or pour into a large zip-top bag, shake until thoroughly mixed.

If you decide to make your own mix, be sure to buy only certified gluten-free flours, as cross-contamination is rampant in mills where gluten is also present. Also, I suggest mixing multiple batches of this recipe at a time, so that you will always have enough on hand; the base recipe yields only 4 cups of mix. Using the flours I list here (not necessarily the alternative flours listed in parentheses, though), there is no need to store the flour in the refrigerator or freezer (these flours have lower fat and protein content, so will not go rancid as easily as some alternative flours).

However, as with any flour, you should store it in airtight containers away from direct sunlight.

Other Gluten-Free Ingredients to Keep on Hand

Baking Powder and Baking Soda

Baking, gluten-free or otherwise, requires a few key staple ingredients. One is a leavening agent. Both baking powder and baking soda are such leavening agents, which is to say that they cause carbon dioxide gas bubbles to form in your recipes, giving rise and open cell structure to baked goods so you are not left with a banana brick when you were hoping for banana bread.

Baking powder is made of baking soda, an acidic ingredient like cream of tartar, and a starch (corn, potato, or wheat) to absorb water and prevent premature gas formation; most brands on the market today are double-acting, so that they react and begin to produce carbon dioxide both when added to moisture as well as when heated while baking. Baking soda requires an acidic ingredient like yogurt, honey, vinegar, buttermilk, or chocolate in a recipe to form carbon dioxide. Some recipes will call for both baking powder and baking soda, whereas others will call for baking powder alone or baking soda alone if an acidic ingredient is also on the ingredient list.

Both baking powder and baking soda lose their potency over time. A good rule of thumb is that they should remain active for twenty-four months from the date of manufacture (which should be printed on the can or box) and be active for three to six months from the date you open the product. Do not use either product if there are lumps in the powder, as this likely indicates that it has been exposed to moisture; for this same reason, do not store them in the refrigerator, or condensation may occur in the container.

If your recipes are not rising as you would like, first look to your leavening agents and determine if they are fresh. Otherwise, you may find that adding an extra ½–1 teaspoon baking powder in your recipe will help, since some gluten-free recipes tend to need an extra lift due to heavier flours or added moisture.

As far as gluten-free brands go, baking soda is gluten-free; most baking powder brands are gluten-free as well and are labeled as such on the container. Commonly available national brands like Rumford, Calumet, Clabber Girl, and Hain Pure Foods Featherweight (potato starch base; corn-free) are all labeled gluten-free. I prefer Rumford and Hain brands, as they are also aluminum-free, but any of these double-acting brands works nicely.

Yeast

Nearly any bread recipe or recipe using a bread dough base, such as cinnamon rolls, requires some kind of yeast. The recipe may also call for another leavening agent like baking powder, but these yeast doughs get most of their lift and open cell structure from yeast—a living micro-organism that feeds on the sugars in a recipe and creates carbon dioxide gas as a by-product. These bubbles of gas are trapped inside the dough as it warms and bakes and forms the open pockets so identified with yeast breads.

I prefer to use rapid rise, fast-acting, or bread machine yeast in my gluten-free yeast bread recipes, whether or not I am using a bread machine. This instant yeast requires only one rise and really doesn't need to be proofed in warm water before adding to a recipe (hence its utility in bread machine baking, although proofing does ensure that your yeast is fresh before ruining a recipe!), cutting the rise time in half and making it especially suited to gluten-free bread recipes that only call for one rise and no punch-down.

As far as instant yeast brands go, Fleischmann's, Red Star, and Hodgson Mill tend to be the most widely available rapid rise yeasts, and they are all gluten-free.

Sugar and Other Sweeteners

Sugar and baking go hand-in-hand. Fortunately, not all sugars are created equally, and some are at least slightly more healthy than others. Cane sugar tends to work best for baking—unrefined, evaporated (crystallized) cane juice is better still, as it retains the flavor from its natural molasses and much of its natural vitamins and minerals. One of my favorite such products is organic cane sugar from Wholesome Sweeteners, which also produces organic light and brown sugar as well as organic Sucanat (made from whole sugar cane)—all of which may be used in recipes calling for brown sugar.

Agave nectar is another wonderful sweetener option. Derived from the agave plant and minimally processed, this raw food is perfect for those requiring a low glycemic diet and those avoiding sugar. Because of agave's recent popularity, brands like Wholesome Sweeteners, Ohgave! and Madhava are now nearly ubiquitous in grocery stores nationwide.

Agave most easily substitutes for honey in recipes, but it is possible to use it in place of granulated sugar by using a measure of agave equal to 75 percent of the sugar called for and reducing the recipe's liquids by 25 to 30 percent. Agave is available in light (a good honey substitute) and dark (a good molasses substitute) varieties and is now seen in flavors ranging from Irish cream to cappuccino. Ohgave! Maple Flavor Agave Syrup is even a wonderful sugar-free option for pancakes!

Agave nectar also has humectant properties that help retain moisture when added to recipes and can help baked goods to stay fresh longer as well. Depending on how much agave is used in a given recipe, you may find that it is best to reduce the oven temperature by 25 degrees and cook longer; also, do not expect crystallization to occur, as is typical in cookie recipes, as agave does not crystallize like sugar.

Xylitol, or sugar alcohol, is another natural, low-calorie, low-glycemic sweetening alternative. It is extracted from plants or tree bark (often from corn, although manufacturer claims indicate that all corn proteins—allergens—are removed in the process) and is typically used in the same ratio as sugar in a recipe (replace 1 cup sugar with 1 cup xylitol), but since xylitol absorbs moisture from recipes, adjustments may need to be made, as necessary. Like other sugar substitutes, if possible, using it in combination with regular sugar will work best, allowing for some caramelization and still giving yeast something to grow on (xylitol will not activate yeast).

Stevia is another sugar alternative recently garnering much attention, as it is a natural, plant-based, no-caloric sweetener. Newer products like Stevia in the Raw offer one-for-one conversions to go from traditional recipes calling for sugar to using stevia in its place. Purists will notice a difference in flavor, and performance is not identical, but especially in quick breads, muffins, and the like, baking with stevia is a nice option for those trying to cut out sugar.

Gluten-Free Oats

Oats were long thought to contain gluten and thus were banned from the diets of celiacs and the gluten sensitive. Further study proved that oats are naturally gluten-free but are contaminated with gluten-containing grains in the fields and during the harvest and milling processes. Companies such as Gluten-Free Oats, Cream Hill Estates, Legacy Valley, and Gifts of Nature all currently produce certified gluten-free oats. If you decide to reintroduce oats into your diet, you'll enjoy not only a delicious ingredient (as oats, oat flour, or oat bran) but also an important source of protein and high-fiber carbohydrates. That high fiber can cause some folks unaccustomed to a high-fiber diet to experience some initial digestive discomfort, so eat oats in smaller quantities (½–¾ cup measured dry oats per day for adults), cooked well, until your body becomes accustomed to the added fiber.

Companies including Legacy Valley and Cream Hill Estates also offer oat flour, which is a great whole-grain, tasty ingredient in breads and even some cookies. It is easy to make your own oat flour though, just choose certified gluten-free oats and grind them in a blender or food processor until fine. If you are searching for an alternative to oats, try substituting with quinoa flakes or rice flakes.

Flax Seeds

Flax seeds are one of my favorite baking ingredients. When ground into a meal, flax seeds add loads of Omega-3s and other essential vitamins and fiber to the diet, offer a delicious nutty taste, can be added to nearly any recipe for a nutritional boost, and can even substitute for eggs in some recipes when mixed with warm water (see Egg Substitute #7, page 16). The flax seeds themselves cannot be digested unless they are ground, so either purchase flaxseed meal or grind it yourself in a blender, food mill (that has never been used for gluten-containing grains), or a food processor.

Even adding just two tablespoons of ground flax seeds to nearly any recipe will enhance the nutrition, flavor, and structure, particularly in breads. Two of my favorite flaxseed companies are Flax USA (they offer golden flax seed) and Carrington Farms. If you are looking to slip a little nutrition into your family's foods and don't want anyone to be the wiser, try golden flax seed instead of the traditional brown variety, which adds suspiciously healthy-looking flecks in breads!

Gluten-Free Cereal and Chips

Many recipes in this book and elsewhere call for breadcrumbs or crushed cereal or chips for breading or as a crunchy topping. While I try to keep a stock of homemade bread in my freezer at all times so that I can always make delicious breadcrumbs (see recipe, page 78), having a stash of gluten-free cereal and chips on hand not only serves as a fantastic alternative ingredient, but is also great to have for munching! Some new and tasty options are available now, but keep looking for new certified gluten-free products on the market each time you shop—the good ones should be in your pantry at all times for recipe or snacking emergencies!

Perhaps the easiest of these to locate is the staple cereal we all remember from our pre-gluten-free days: Chex cereal. Chex recently embraced the gluten-free community by reformulating their ingredients, opting for molasses instead of malt, thus rendering most of their varieties gluten-free. Now available are Rice, Corn, Honey Nut, Chocolate, and Cinnamon flavors, all of which are gluten-free. Rice and Corn Chex are great crunchy toppings for casseroles (see Macaroni and Cheese, page 150) or coatings (see Fish Sticks, page 148) or fillers (see Crab Cakes, page 143). Choosing a sweeter variety can help make the flavors of munchies like Party Mix your own (see page 90).

As for chips, many traditional corn chips are certified gluten-free; if you prefer more whole grains in your chips, definitely try brands like Food Should Taste Good Multi-Grain Chips. These are fantastic for munching, dipping, or crunching into toppings and coatings (see recipes above).

Egg Substitutes

Substituting for eggs in baking is often no easy feat. Eggs can provide stick-to-it-ness, body, and loft and also boost flavor in lots of recipes, not to mention increase the protein of the end result. If you find that eggs need to leave your diet for whatever reason, though, take heart! There are several very viable options, you just need to understand their limitations.

One trick to transforming many recipes to egg-free is to choose the right pan. Remember that many quick breads, muffins, and cakes will not have the same structural integrity without real eggs, so cheat a little bit and give your recipe more support by using smaller pans. In many recipes where a full loaf will be too soggy or will collapse without eggs, muffins, mini-loaves, or even mini-muffins will be perfect, even without the eggs! The same holds true for cakes—opt for cupcakes for the best results. Metal pans also help in baking, so be sure to have the right pan on hand to make your life easier.

Before we delve into egg substitutions, bear in mind that if any given recipe calls for more than two eggs, reconsider if you really must try it egg-free. Quiches, angel food cake, custards . . . these recipes are founded on eggs. Replacing them makes the recipe *completely* different, which is not to say that the results will be bad, just don't expect them to taste or have the texture of the original egg version.

Much like gluten-free flour, there is not one stand-alone egg substitution that equally replaces eggs in every style recipe. One exception is duck eggs. Some folks may tolerate duck eggs (as opposed to chicken eggs found in the grocery store), which can often be found from local farmers or co-operatives in your area. If you can tolerate duck eggs, they will work as a good substitute for any recipe calling for eggs, so long as they are "large" size, since most recipes contemplate this size egg.

Most recipes (mine included) call for large eggs, not medium or extra large eggs. With that in mind, see below for several large egg substitution products and recipes, as well as their most successful applications.

Egg-Free Mayonnaise

Egg-free mayonnaise dressings help bring lots of salads, baked goods, and casseroles back to the table for those avoiding eggs. Look for Follow Your Heart Vegenaise and Nasoya Nayonaise as reliable and readily available alternatives for these recipes.

Ener-G Egg Replacer

BEST FOR: COOKIES, CAKES, AND QUICK BREADS

For egg replacement in recipes calling for two or fewer eggs, there are a gaggle of options. The simplest is to use Ener-G egg replacer. It is gluten- and egg-free, containing only potato starch, tapioca starch flour, leavening (calcium lactate [not derived from dairy], calcium carbonate, and citric acid), sodium carboxymethylcellulose, and methylcellulose. Thus, the manufacturer states that this product is free of gluten, wheat, casein, dairy, egg, yeast, soys, nut, and rice.

Although the product is billed as a substitution for a full egg, egg white, or egg yolk, I personally do not like its performance as an egg yolk substitute, largely because this egg substitute is fat-free and yolks are largely comprised of fat. In recipes calling for yolks, try supplementing Ener-G egg replacer with 1 teaspoon canola oil to improve the texture of your dish.

Recipes that tend to work best with this product are those like cookies, cakes, and quick breads. I find that this substitute works best when whipped together with water until frothy (in proportions according to product directions) in a food processor, in a blender, or with a hand mixer before adding to a recipe. For cookies made using this or any egg replacer, make sure that the dough is quite cold (refrigerated overnight is best) before working with it.

Homemade Egg Replacers

BEST FOR: QUICK BREADS, CAKES, BROWNIES, AND SOME COOKIES

Other homemade egg substitutes that also work well in quick breads, cakes, brownies, and some cookies include these homemade versions (mix all ingredients of each substitute together well before adding to recipe). Each recipe below equals one full large egg:

Egg Substitute #1:

1 tablespoon milk powder (dairy, soy, or DariFree)
1 tablespoon cornstarch
2 tablespoons warm water

Egg Substitute #2:

1 tablespoon canola oil
2 tablespoons water
2 teaspoons gluten-free baking powder

Egg Substitute #3:

¼ cup yogurt (dairy, soy, or coconut work best)

Egg Substitute #4:

3 tablespoons egg-free mayonnaise (see page 14 for brands)

Egg Substitute # 5:

¼ cup firm or extra firm silken tofu, blended in a food processor or blender with ½ teaspoon gluten-free baking powder

BEST FOR: QUICK BREADS, BROWNIES, AND PANCAKES

Another wonderful option for an egg substitute, particularly in quick breads, brownies, and pancakes, is to use fruit puree. If you find the results too heavy, modify by adding ¼–½ teaspoon gluten-free baking powder for each egg substituted.

Egg Substitute # 6:

¼ cup mashed, very ripe bananas, apple puree, apple butter, applesauce,
or canned pumpkin

BEST FOR: QUICK BREADS, YEAST BREADS, BATTERS, AND SOME COOKIES

One of my favorite egg replacers for cookies (such as oatmeal-raisin), quick breads, pancakes, and yeast breads in particular is flaxseed meal. You can buy flax seeds (golden or brown) and grind them into meal for this use or purchase the meal ready-ground. Store flaxseed meal in your refrigerator, as its high protein and oil content will cause it to go rancid quickly otherwise. Don't use whole flax seeds, as these will neither offer the viscous binding properties of egg, nor the nutritional benefits of the flaxseed meal (see "Flax Seeds," page 12).

Once the flaxseed meal is added to the water, stir and allow it to gel before adding it to your recipe; you can speed this process along by warming over low heat until a viscous liquid is formed.

Egg Substitute #7:

1 tablespoon flaxseed meal
3 tablespoons very warm water

FOR SAVORY RECIPES

In many savory recipes, enhance the flavors of the dish by using complementary ingredients as binders to replace the eggs.

Egg (Savory) Substitute #8:

¼ cup firm or extra firm silken tofu, blended in a food processor or blender with ½ teaspoon gluten-free baking powder

Egg (Savory) Substitute #9:

¼ cup mashed potatoes, gluten-free oats, tomato paste, or gluten-free breadcrumbs

BEST FOR: REPLACING EGG YOLK

For egg yolk substitutes, try one of these recipes to equal two egg yolks.

Egg (Yolk) Substitute #10:

¼ cup silken tofu, blended in a food processor or blender

Egg (Yolk) Substitute #11:

3 tablespoons egg-free mayonnaise (see page 14 for brands) (not fat-free)

Egg (Yolk) Substitute #12

WHISK TOGETHER, THEN SET ASIDE TO STEEP UNTIL VISCOUS:

1 tablespoon flaxseed meal (use golden flaxseed meal in recipes like cookies so it's not apparent in the dough)

2 tablespoons hot water

2 teaspoons canola oil

BEST FOR: FRYING FOODS AND BROWNING CRUSTS

For other egg uses, such as adhering breadcrumbs or flour to foods before frying or brushing on pie crusts and breads before baking, try using an equal amount of your milk of choice.

Dairy and Soy Substitutes

The most common food sensitivity is to dairy products; in fact, current estimates classify fully 60–70 percent of the world's adult population as lactose (milk sugar) intolerant.* Fortunately, there are more and more dairy-free ingredients added to the market each day, leaving us lots of options! Soy is the most ubiquitous dairy alternative, appearing in everything from soy sour cream to soy cream cheese. Fortunately for those who also avoid soy, coconut and rice have begun to turn up as yogurt and ice cream bases, offering great ingredient options in baking.

Milk

In any recipe calling for milk, a one-for-one substitution with one of the many non-skim dairy-free milks would work. The best in baking are soy, coconut, or nut milks like almond, due to their higher protein and fat content, which lend more body to recipes. Hemp milk has slightly less protein, and rice milk—although a nearly allergen-free alternative—has very low protein and is quite watery, so should not be your first choice for baking. If using rice milk in baking, add one egg yolk for every cup of rice milk. While oat milk is an attractive option, it may not be certified gluten-free, so be aware of the likelihood of cross-contamination in production.

Buttermilk

Even before I went dairy-free, I used to find recipes I wanted to try that called for buttermilk, but I never seemed to have this ingredient on hand. The absolute easiest

----

*An estimated 30–50 million American adults are lactose intolerant, with certain population groups—including Asians, African Americans, American Indians, and Hispanics—manifesting intolerance in 80–100 percent of their population. National Institute of Diabetes and Digestive and Kidney Diseases, National Institutes of Health, "Digestive Disease Statistics," retrieved April 25, 2010, from http://digestive.niddk.nih.gov/statistics/statistics.htm; www.nichd.nih.gov/publications/pubs/ . . . /NICHD_MM_Lactose_FS.pdf.

fix was to simply add 1 tablespoon lemon juice to each cup of milk. The beauty of its simplicity holds true for nondairy milks as well:

1 cup buttermilk = 1 cup nondairy milk + 1 tablespoon lemon juice (let stand until curdled before using).

Half-and-Half or Heavy Cream

Recipes requiring half-and-half often work well with liquid nondairy creamer instead. Soy and coconut creamers are readily available at organic markets, if not at your local grocer, and they are often flavored. For a recipe calling for half-and-half, stick with plain or vanilla nondairy creamer. If a recipe calls for heavy cream, there are even nondairy options for that: Mimic Creme is one alternative to cream and is vegan, gluten-free, and soy-free.

Evaporated Milk

Evaporated milk is nothing more than milk that is 60 percent concentrated; nondairy milk powder works as a good substitute when making a homemade version. This simple recipe opens up options for loads of fun recipes like dairy-free soufflés and fudge!

Nondairy Evaporated Milk

MAKES APPROXIMATELY 1 CUP

½ cup nondairy milk powder (I prefer DariFree Vitamin Enriched, Fat-Free, Non-Dairy Milk Alternative)
1 cup hot water

▸ In a large bowl, stir in and dissolve the nondairy milk powder in hot water.

▸ Allow the mixture to cool before using in your recipes; store unused mixture in a sealed container in the refrigerator for use in another recipe (use within a week).

Sweetened Condensed Milk

Sweetened condensed milk is simply a quantity of evaporated milk plus approximately 1½ times that amount of granulated sugar. I prefer DariFree Original Powder as the dairy-free base for this recipe.

Sweetened Condensed Milk

MAKES APPROXIMATELY 1½ CUPS

½ cup DariFree
1 cup hot water
1½ cups granulated cane sugar

▸ In a large saucepan, dissolve the nondairy milk powder in the hot water. Once fully dissolved, stir in the sugar over medium heat and stir periodically until the sugar is fully dissolved and the milk has thickened quite a bit.

▸ Allow the mixture to cool before using in your recipes; store unused mixture in a sealed container in the refrigerator for use in another recipe (use within a week).

Yogurt and Sour Cream

Yogurt is another big baking ingredient, and whether you like to eat yogurt by itself or not, it can be very valuable in your recipes. Yogurt and sour cream are nearly interchangeable in recipes, and there are soy yogurt and sour cream products available now in nearly every grocery store (look for Tofutti Better than Sour Cream and Follow Your Heart Soy Sour Cream). Both ingredients add stable moisture to recipes like quick breads, for example, keeping them from drying out as quickly after baking.

In baking recipes, look to flavored yogurts to enhance the taste of the dish as well. Specialty markets will offer greater variety, including coconut and rice yogurts (look for brands like So Delicious). I do not prefer rice yogurts in my baking, as they tend to be more watery, but they are a viable option for those whose food restrictions prevent them from choosing another source for these ingredients.

If you are avoiding dairy and soy, in a recipe calling for sour cream, I suggest opting for coconut yogurt instead—it tastes great and is a welcome option for those living dairy- and soy-free!

Butter and Shortening

Butter is another common dairy product for which there are very good substitutes. Stay away from products labeled "spreads" wherever possible, as these products are designed to spread smoothly on breads, so they have a high moisture content; used as a baking ingredient, this attribute will cause many of your baked goods to spread as well. My personal favorite for baking is Earth Balance Buttery Sticks. All natural, dairy-free, and vegan, it also uses no hydrogenated oils and contains no trans fats, but it does contain soy. It acts and tastes so much like butter, that I use it in nearly all my dairy-free baking.

Ghee, or Indian clarified butter, is a butter substitute that offers a rich flavor and doesn't smoke or burn at high heats when frying. Although the description sounds like ghee would contain "dairy," the clarification process actually removes milk solids like lactose and casein, leaving the healthy butter fats behind. It is considered therefore lactose and casein-free, but check the reasons for your dietary restrictions against this product to see if it is right for you.

Another option is to simply substitute vegetable shortening for butter in recipes. I often use a combination of the two (in cookies and pie crusts, in particular), as having two different ingredients that melt at different rates can help to make them flakier and hold together better. Two very good options for vegetable shortening are Earth Balance Shortening Sticks and Spectrum palm oil shortening, the latter also being soy-free.

If you are avoiding soy as well as dairy, Earth Balance also makes a Buttery Spread, which has the added benefit of tasting much like butter and is soy- and dairy-free, but it is still a "spread" and therefore only works well in certain recipes (like my Graham Crackers, page 212); it works best when very cold.

Still another good option is coconut oil, which is actually firm at room temperature, like a shortening. This fat substitute has no cholesterol and has a pleasant taste, unlike traditional shortening which is tasteless. Coconut oil can be a great option for frying and baking.

Finally, consider this fat-free option: substitute 6 tablespoons unsweetened applesauce or pumpkin puree for each ½ cup of butter required in a recipe. This substitution works best in quick breads and will cause the end result to be denser, but that result is not necessarily bad, just different.

Cheese and Cream Cheese

Cheese, including cream cheese, has come a long way in its dairy-free incarnations. It is currently possible to find dairy-free cheeses of many varieties to suit nearly any recipe. I often make dairy-free pizzas and use mixtures of various dairy-free cheeses with yummy results. Soy- and dairy-free, some of my favorite shredded cheeses are made by Daiya—they currently offer Cheddar Style and Mozzarella Style. Galaxy

Nutritional Foods also makes Veggie, Vegan, Rice, and Rice Vegan cheeses in many flavor varieties to suit most diets, including cheddar, pepper jack, mozzarella, and Parmesan. Eat in the Raw Parma is yet another Parmesan alternative that is actually made from walnuts, nutritional yeast, and sea salt. Nutritional yeast on its own makes a nice (and nutritious!) Parmesan alternative.

Depending on the reason for your dairy avoidance, be careful with some of the other alternative cheeses, though, as many actually contain cow's milk protein, called casein. If your specific allergy is to cow's milk or to casein, look for the many wonderful goat's milk offerings available. Goat's milk contains different casein, as well as lactose, though. Many people who are not lactose intolerant but are sensitive to cow's milk products can more easily digest goat's milk, opening up a host of ingredient possibilities.

Companies like Tofutti (Better than Cream Cheese), Follow Your Heart (Cream Cheese Alternative), and others make various flavors of soy cream cheese, and the plain flavor makes a cheesecake no one would ever suspect of being dairy-free (see page 191)!

Ice Cream and Whipped Cream

Ice cream is a wonderful dessert by itself or as a complement to many pies, cookies, and other treats. Soy, coconut, and even hemp ice creams are abundantly found in most grocers' freezer cases, in an ever-expanding array of flavors. You can also try your hand at making your own ice cream using ingredients that suit your tastes and dietary sensitivities. The same goes for whipped cream, but you may also want to try the ready-made soy whipped creams like Soyatoo! Soy Whip and Rice Whip, which are available at most specialty food stores.

Nut Substitutes

Avoiding nuts in restaurants and processed foods can sometimes be tricky, although as with any food allergy, it is much simpler when cooking at home. Since nuts are on the FDA's eight most prevalent food allergens list, you can rely on the FDA-mandated food allergy statements on ingredient labels (e.g., "contains nuts"), but I always suggest contacting manufacturers about their cross-contamination prevention protocols when nuts are present in their manufacturing facility. Especially if you avoid only peanuts *or* tree nuts, but not both, there are many more food options that ought to be open to you. Contact manufacturers of alternative nut products to ensure their cross-contamination procedures meet your expectations. For example, if you avoid only peanuts, and would like to use almond butter, contact the almond butter manufacturers to ensure that there is no possibility of peanut contamination in their facility.

As far as nut substitutes go, it all depends on the recipe. Certainly many recipes use nuts as an added and optional flavor that can simply be left out (think chocolate chip cookies with chopped nuts). Other recipes seemingly rely on nuts as a main ingredient, like party mixes made up primarily of pretzels and nuts. In these instances, it often works well to use various seeds in place of nuts to provide the roasted flavor and crunchy texture that the nuts would have brought to the recipe. Pumpkin seeds and sunflower seeds are some of my favorites, but soy "nuts" or edamame also offer a great crunch, nutritional benefits, and salty punch to many dishes.

So, decide which characteristic is important in the recipe you are looking to render nut-free and look to these substitutes to guide your way to a nearly indistinguishable substitution!

Nutty Texture

Ground seeds (flax seeds, sunflower, poppy, sesame, pumpkin): grind them as finely as the recipe recommends for nuts

Crushed gluten-free cereal (cornflakes, crispy rice cereal, etc.)

Crushed gluten-free corn or potato chips

Nutty Taste

Sunflower "nut" butter or soy "nut" butter

Flaxseed meal

Maple syrup or flavoring: no, it's not nutty, but it provides that subtle undertone in a recipe that needs oomph from an ingredient like almond extract

Toasted coconut: grind as finely as you would have ground the nuts

Peanut Butter

In recipes like peanut butter cookies, peanut butter frosting, peanut butter cake, peanut butter candy, you might think there is just no substitute. But think again! I have made all of these recipes using soy "nut" butter or sunflower "nut" butter in place of peanut butter with amazing results! The texture of these products is often runnier than common peanut butter, but it is very similar to "natural" or fresh ground peanut butter. If peanuts are the only nuts you must avoid, look to almond butter or cashew butter as wonderful recipe alternatives as well. Prior to using, be sure to stir any layers of oil into the product to make an even consistency. You may also need to adjust for its added moisture in any of your existing recipes (I've already compensated for it in the recipes in this book where noted), but the end result will look, smell, and taste just as good as any peanut butter concoction ever could!

Alcohols in Baking

Although distilled alcohols are rendered gluten-free through the distillation process, even if they are made using grains containing gluten, it is wise to check with each manufacturer to determine if any gluten has been added for flavoring after distillation. I like to use some distilled liquor and liqueurs in my baking for flavoring (see my Pumpkin Pie recipe, page 226), but feel free to substitute fruit juices and ciders, as noted, if you prefer.

Another often overlooked ingredient in baking is beer. Until recently, there were little to no options for gluten-free beer, so it was easy to pass this ingredient by. We are now lucky enough to have many options, from the offerings of small microbreweries to traditional Belgian ales, all made gluten-free using alternative grains like sorghum and millet. Some of these beers are quite frankly indistinguishable from their traditional counterparts, and others require some getting used to.

My favorites for baking—and you'll see notes in the recipes where I use these—are made in Belgium by Green's beers. The three offerings currently imported to the United States include a Blonde, an Amber, and a Dubbel Dark variety. Each imparts a different subtle flavor to recipes like tempura, yeast bread, and chocolate cake that should not be overlooked. These underlying aromas and flavors, combined with their carbonation, help to create light and airy creations that are full of flavor without being sickeningly sweet. Hence, the tempura batter is lacy and crisp; the chocolate cake is feather-light and subtle enough to eat a whole piece without having to lie down afterward! If you don't have these beers in your area, ask your local store to carry them so you can taste for yourself—otherwise, feel free to substitute for these ingredients with other carbonated liquids like ginger ale or Perrier.

When using flavor extracts in baking, such as vanilla, peppermint, or almond, always choose those that are pure, not imitation flavorings. These extracts will contain alcohols, but they should be gluten-free when they are pure, and many brands are actually labeled as such. One of my favorite brands for both purity of taste and certified gluten-free ingredients is Nielsen-Massey Vanillas. McCormick spices and extracts are also all currently gluten-free, although as with any product, always check current product labels before purchasing to be sure that the company has not changed ingredient formulas.

ABOUT THE ICONS

Icons delineate when a recipe does not include—or may successfully be made free from—a certain food allergen ingredient. Consult the substitution guide (pages 5–25) for suggestions on how to make substitutions for these food allergens as needed.

GF = Gluten-Free

Every recipe in this book is naturally gluten-free or is rendered gluten-free by using gluten-free flours, as described herein.

D = Dairy-Free

All of the recipes in this book are naturally dairy-free or can be made dairy-free by using specified nondairy substitutes.

N = Nut-Free

Each recipe in this book is naturally nut-free or may be made nut-free by omitting nuts or using nut alternatives.

S = Soy-Free

Soy-free options are available for recipes with this designation. Most recipes in this book are soy-free or can be made soy-free.

E = Egg-Free

When this icon is used, the recipe is either egg-free or can be made egg-free by using an appropriate egg substitute. Most recipes in this book are egg-free or can be made egg-free.

V = Vegetarian (not necessarily vegan)

Most recipes in this book are already vegetarian; a few recipes contemplate using fish, chicken, or shellfish, but all recipes may be made without using shellfish, as called out in the recipe ingredients.

Baking Notes

One of the benefits of teaching cooking classes all over the country is that I hear about baking issues and concerns from folks . . . all over the country! I try to take these questions back to my own kitchen and resolve them so that I can help others bake more successfully, one of the primary reasons for this book.

An issue that seems to plague bakers everywhere (regardless of the recipe or food ingredient restriction) is contending with ovens that all bake differently. I have even had inconsistent results with my professional-grade oven, so I know how frustrating this problem can be!

I've outlined general baking parameters in each recipe, but particularly with quick breads, always test for doneness with a skewer or cake tester inserted into the middle of each loaf or a muffin to be sure it's pretty clean before removing it from the oven (I keep a stash of wooden skewers in a drawer next to my oven for just this purpose). Using a convection setting, if your oven has one, is also a good way to ensure more even baking with muffins, breads, and cakes, so opt for those settings if you can. With yeast breads, a baking thermometer is an invaluable tool to ensure your breads are fully cooked in the middle (never remove your loaf until the internal temperature is 205–210°F!). There is no substitute for common sense in baking, so go with your instincts, too—if the baked good smells done and looks done, it probably is!

The other area of primary concern for bakers of all skill levels is yeast breads. Compounding the fear level of home and commercial bakers alike is the prospect of baking yeast breads without gluten. If your knees begin to knock at the thought of trying to make gluten-free bread from scratch, you are not alone! But just because so many companies are producing rock-hard or rubbery loaves and calling them "gluten-free bread" does not mean that it is impossible to make great gluten-free bread at home.

I have consulted with and spoken to hundreds of professional bakers at events where successfully making gluten-free breads was my keynote address. I tell them what I'm about to tell you: in many ways, working with gluten-free yeast dough is actually *easier* than working with dough that contains gluten. . . . It's true. The very thing that makes gluten-containing dough work so well with yeast (gluten gives it elasticity and helps to form the structure around the air pockets that holds the bread's shape) also makes it time-consuming and tricky to work with.

In contrast, gluten-free yeast doughs—if made with the proper flours and gums to mimic the elasticity of gluten—should *not* be kneaded, exercised, punched down, or even given additional rises. Those exhausting and time-consuming steps actually dry out and deflate gluten-free doughs. Thus, a proper gluten-free loaf of bread cooks in half or one-third the time of a regular gluten-containing loaf, without any skillful kneading steps! (This is the part where you say "Yay!" Celebrate our victories where they come!)

Start with these recipes, using the flours described, and you'll gain confidence in the world of gluten-free yeast breads. Once you're making homemade pizza like a champ, your family is clamoring for your famous cinnamon sticky rolls, and you're serving up amazing French toast with your homemade sandwich bread, you'll have harnessed the secret of gluten-free bread baking . . . and you don't have to tell anyone how easy it really is!

If you have any less-than-stellar results along the way, never fear! Consider that you're saving up for next Thanksgiving's stuffing or the breading for your next batch of fish sticks. Preserve any less-than-perfect experimental loaves by storing them in zip-top bags in your freezer to convert later into stuffing cubes or breadcrumbs and you'll be saving time and money by recycling for other recipes. It's all in how you approach it; once you find a recipe that produces results you love, you'll be glad you have a backup store of these leftovers so you don't have to make them from scratch when you really need some tasty breadcrumbs for crab cakes or croutons for your gazpacho!

Some of these recipes offer directions for using a bread machine. If you are inclined to purchase a bread maker, I suggest buying a brand that offers a specific "gluten-free bread" setting, or at least has a setting with only one rise and no punch-down of the dough. Some good brands include Breadman, Cuisinart, and Zojirushi. A bread machine can be a real time-saver, but it is certainly not required to make delicious gluten-free bread. However, if you are not using a bread maker, a stand mixer is a near necessity. Some bread dough is extremely thick and would be virtually impossible to mix well with a hand mixer, opt for mixing by hand instead.

Another handy tool to have in your arsenal when baking bread is an instant-read thermometer with a probe to test the internal temperature of your loaves and help determine when they are fully cooked. Somewhere between 200°F and 210°F is usually about right. If you don't have a thermometer, you can still check for how much humidity remains inside the loaf the old-fashioned way—by thumping it. When it sounds hollow, the humidity is baked out, and it is done.

One final note on measurements. The recipes in this book are written for the home baker in mind. Most home bakers do not own food scales, so the recipes are written using volumetric measurements (i.e., cups, teaspoons, and so on). This method is imprecise, however, as sifting flour, scooping flour, or pouring flour, for example, may each ultimately result in a different measurement (for the record, I recommend scooping the flour into a measuring cup without packing).

If you try a recipe and find that it is too wet, try it again and add a bit more flour; too dry, remove some flour. Baking—particularly gluten-free baking—is all about trial and error. Rarely will you get results that are worse than most of the prepackaged foods on the market; just take notes and try the recipe a bit differently next time. The good news here is that you get to eat your mistakes!

So let's get on to baking some yummy foods!

PART II

The Recipes

ABOUT THE RECIPES

Free for All Cooking represents the culmination of my many years of working with those whose diets are restricted by gluten—and more. More than ten years ago now, I was diagnosed with celiac disease, and my own struggles to find foods I could enjoy as a celiac, lactose-intolerant pescatarian who loved to entertain and share family meals led me to share my solutions with others in my first cookbook, *Nearly Normal Cooking for Gluten-Free Eating*. This first book was a collection of many of my own family's favorite dishes made gluten-free.

Since publishing that book, I have heard from countless readers seeking to alter recipes to accommodate additional dietary restrictions. I have also taught cooking classes around the country to people who need far more recipe modifications than just gluten-free, and I have consulted with individuals possessing every possible dietary restriction. That work, combined with the research that went into the publication of my second book, *The First Year: Celiac Disease and Living Gluten-Free*, proved to me the need for a cookbook dedicated to all of us who struggle with more than just gluten-free cooking.

Addressing the many additional dietary restrictions my clients and readers have shared with me has become the challenge I have so enjoyed helping others to overcome.

With *Free for All Cooking*, it is my intent to arm you with solutions for your family's own particular set of ingredient restrictions. Many of these recipes are comfort foods from my childhood or are close approximations to what I remember enjoying in my pre-gluten-free days. Others are newer recipes I have developed and shared with my weekly recipe newsletter subscribers over the last couple of years; still others are brand-new ones I have never shared before. This new compendium covers everything from appetizers to desserts, and as always, my recipes use common ingredients and few steps—gluten-free made easy!

With determination and creativity, nearly any recipe can be crafted to accommodate nearly every dietary restriction. Nearly. I say this because there are obvious foods like steak that are never going to be vegetarian, and there are somewhat less obvious foods like angel food cake that are never going to be egg-free. With that in mind, though, assess the dietary restrictions with which you are working and shift your perspective a little when you think about a recipe you are craving. Rather than looking at certain recipes as off-limits due to a food restriction, look at them as opportunities for you to get creative.

Because there are so many different potential combinations, this book will show you how to modify recipes and apply certain substitutions to suit your own needs, *without removing other potential allergen ingredients that you otherwise could eat*. So, if you must avoid gluten, dairy, and peanuts, for example, but may still eat eggs, soy, shellfish, and fish, this book can help. In this way, the book is more of a guidebook than a cookbook. These recipes are written with as much flexibility as is possible, so that most may be made with all the ingredients you can still enjoy.

Each recipe in this book includes icons that indicate the specific ingredients without which it may be made: gluten; dairy; nuts; soy; eggs; or vegetarian (not necessarily vegan). By self-selecting the items that you need to avoid and turning to the section called "Ingredients: A Handy Substitution Guide" that begins on page 5, you can fashion the recipe to suit your particular needs safely, easily, and deliciously.

In addition to being gluten-free, each recipe in this book can be made dairy-free, as that diet is required for so many celiacs, those following a gluten-free/casein-free

(GFCF) diet, and others, including the majority of the general population who is lactose intolerant. However, if you may include dairy in your diet, feel free to substitute dairy products like butter and cow's milk where nondairy ingredients are listed.

With a few exceptions, most of the recipes in this book can be made without eggs. And although I typically use soy ingredients in my own baking so that the recipes may be made dairy-free, I suggest alternatives here to render most any recipe soy-free as well. Nearly all of these recipes are nut-free; the ones that do call for nuts may still be made deliciously without adding them. Where shellfish are included, I offer substitutes for those as well.

Obviously, there are other potential allergens that may not be covered by these recipes. Unfortunately, it is simply impossible to conceive of every possible combination of allergens and account for them in every recipe. I have tried to address the most prevalent food allergens in this book.

My hope is that you find these recipes liberating, in contrast to restrictions you may have been feeling due to your food sensitivities. The ingredient substitution guide on page 5 can also help you return to most any favorite recipes you've enjoyed in the past. Applying these ingredient rules can allow you to once again make many of those recipes safely as well.

Where helpful, I list specific brands of products to assist you in shopping. However, you still must double-check that manufacturers have not changed ingredient formulations or manufacturing processes over time. Fortunately, though, new products are being offered every day, so be sure to keep an eye out for new choices.

If you still find yourself stumbling over other food limitations, I urge you to go back to basics and focus on the many healthful, unprocessed foods provided by Mother Nature herself. It never hurts to be reminded to eat more fruits and vegetables! While many of the recipes offered here are indeed for baked goods (the kind of recipes requiring the most modifications to accommodate food allergies and sensitivities), we could all afford to eat more of the wonderful and nutritious foods that are and have always been gluten- and largely allergy-free.

1

Breakfast Foods

Applesauce-Oat Muffins

Here's a great way to add more healthy oats to your diet! These bake up moist, thanks to the applesauce, and the oats give them a hearty look and a great texture.

½ cup granulated cane sugar

½ cup butter or nondairy alternative, room temperature

2 large eggs or egg substitute of choice (like Ener-G Egg Replacer or Egg Substitute #1, 2, 6, or 7, pages 15–16)

1 cup unsweetened applesauce

½ cup vanilla yogurt (dairy or nondairy)

2 cups Jules Gluten Free All Purpose Flour (pages 6, 8)

1 teaspoon baking soda

2 teaspoons baking powder, gluten-free

2 tablespoons flaxseed meal (optional, but recommended)

¼ cup certified gluten-free oats

1½ teaspoons cinnamon

½ teaspoon nutmeg

½ cup baking raisins (or boil raisins in water, drain, then add to the recipe)

Cinnamon-sugar mixture for the tops

Extra certified gluten-free oats for the tops

▸ Preheat the oven to 350°F (static) or 325°F (convection).

▸ Oil or line muffin cups and set aside (makes approximately 15 regular-size muffins or 48 mini-muffins).

▸ Combine the sugar and butter in a large mixing bowl, beating until fluffy. Add in the eggs, applesauce, and yogurt and mix well.

▸ In a separate bowl, whisk together all the dry ingredients. Gradually add them into the wet ingredients and beat until incorporated. Stir in the raisins last.

▸ Fill muffin cups to two-thirds full and sprinkle cinnamon-sugar mixture and oats on top.

▸ Bake for 15–20 minutes for mini-muffins, 25–30 minutes for regular-size muffins. Transfer to a wire rack to cool completely.

MAKES APPROXIMATELY 15 REGULAR-SIZE MUFFINS OR 48 MINI-MUFFINS

Banana Blueberry Muffins

If bananas didn't disappear so quickly in my house—the same goes for blueberries—I'd probably make these every week! Tip: buy the discounted, over-ripe bananas and peel and freeze them so you have them on hand when you're hankering for these!

> ½ cup butter or nondairy alternative
> ½ cup granulated cane sugar
> 2 large eggs or egg substitute of choice (like Ener-G Egg Replacer or Egg Substitute #1, 2, 6, or 7, pages 15–16)
> 1 teaspoon vanilla extract, gluten-free
> ½ cup sour cream (dairy or nondairy) or plain coconut yogurt
> 1 cup mashed ripe banana (approximately 2 bananas)
> 1½ cups Jules Gluten Free All Purpose Flour (pages 6, 8)
> 1 teaspoon baking soda
> 2 teaspoons baking powder, gluten-free
> ½ teaspoon salt
> 2 teaspoons cinnamon
> 3 tablespoons flaxseed meal (optional, but recommended)
> 1½ cups fresh or frozen blueberries

▸ Preheat the oven to 350°F (static) or 325°F (convection).

▸ Oil or line muffin cups and set aside (makes approximately 16 muffins).

▸ Cream the butter and sugar until the mixture is light and fluffy. Add the eggs and vanilla and beat well.

▸ Mix in the sour cream and banana until well blended.

▸ In a separate bowl, whisk together all the dry ingredients then add them gradually into the wet mixture until thoroughly mixed. Lastly, gently stir in the blueberries.

▸ Spoon the batter into oiled muffin tins, filling two-thirds full. Bake for 30 minutes or until lightly browned.

▸ Cool before removing from tins.

MAKES APPROXIMATELY 16 MUFFINS

See photo insert.

Chai Teacakes

Chai tea is so delicious that I thought it would be a wonderful addition to these breakfast cakes. Yummy, flavorful, and healthy—definitely worth a try on a chilly winter morning!

¼ cup granulated cane sugar

4 tablespoons honey or light agave nectar

6 tablespoons butter or nondairy alternative

2 large eggs or egg substitute of choice (like Ener-G Egg Replacer or Egg Substitute #1, 2, 3, 4, or 7, pages 15–16), beaten

1 banana, mashed, or ¼ cup unsweetened applesauce

½ cup prepared chai tea latte (prepare or brew according to package directions)

1 cup Jules Gluten Free All Purpose Flour (pages 6, 8)

½ cup brown rice flour, buckwheat flour, or Jules Gluten Free All Purpose Flour

2 teaspoons baking powder, gluten-free

½ teaspoon baking soda

¼ teaspoon salt

1½ teaspoons pumpkin pie spice

▸ Coat 12 muffin tins with cooking oil. Preheat the oven to 325°F (convection) or 350°F (static).

▸ Beat the sugar, honey, and butter until light and fluffy. Blend in the remaining wet ingredients (eggs, banana, and chai). In a separate bowl, whisk together the dry ingredients. Gradually pour the dry ingredients into the wet ingredient bowl while mixing until smooth.

▸ Fill the muffin tins two-thirds full and bake until they are light brown, approximately 15 minutes for mini-muffins or 20–30 minutes for regular muffins.

MAKES 12 REGULAR-SIZE MUFFINS OR 24 MINI-MUFFINS

Cinnamon Buns

Is it just me, or do we all have a serious connection to cinnamon buns in our past? The smell of these alone can satisfy (okay, not really satisfy . . . but close!). These buns aren't difficult to make, but they will impress anyone who smells them baking (and is lucky enough to get one).

DOUGH:

2 cups Jules Gluten Free All Purpose Flour (see pages 6, 8)

¼ cup milk powder (dairy or nondairy)

½ teaspoon baking soda

2 teaspoons baking powder, gluten-free

1 teaspoon cinnamon

¼ cup shortening

1 cup vanilla yogurt (dairy or nondairy)

3 tablespoons honey or agave nectar

2 eggs or egg substitute of choice (like Egg Substitute #1, 2, or 7, pages 15–16)

1 teaspoon apple cider vinegar

2¼ teaspoons (1 packet) rapid rise yeast, gluten-free

TOPPING:

4 tablespoons melted butter (dairy or nondairy) (to brush onto the raw dough)

2 tablespoons melted butter (dairy or nondairy)

½ cup granulated cane sugar

2 teaspoons cinnamon

¾ cup raisins or other dried berries (optional)

ICING (OPTIONAL):

1 cup sifted confectioner's sugar

¼ teaspoon vanilla extract, gluten-free

2–4 tablespoons milk (dairy or nondairy) or orange juice (just enough added to make a drizzling consistency)

continues

- In a large bowl, whisk together the dry ingredients, except yeast. Cut the shortening into small pieces and cut into the dry ingredients with a dough paddle attachment on an electric mixer or a pastry cutter by hand.

- In a smaller bowl, stir together the wet ingredients until combined. Slowly add the liquid mixture to the dry ingredient bowl, mix with the paddle attachment, and pour in the yeast, stirring until the lumps are removed from the dough. Beat an additional 1–2 minutes thereafter.

- Dust a clean counter or pastry mat and your hands with gluten-free flour or cornstarch. Grab small fistfuls of the wet dough, rolling it gently under your fingertips in flour and gently shaping each ball of dough into a log (dough will be very sticky). Brush off any excess flour using a pastry brush. Transfer the logs to a baking sheet lined with parchment paper.

- Gently and loosely wind up one end of each log in concentric circles around itself to shape the bun (leave a small bit of space between each circle to allow the dough to rise). Brush melted butter over all exposed areas of the dough. In a small bowl, mix together the melted butter, cinnamon, and sugar topping with a fork, then crumble the topping and raisins (if using) over and in the spaces between each circle. Repeat with all buns.

- Cover the buns with wax paper sprayed with cooking oil and let rise for 30 minutes in a warm location like a warming drawer or a 200°F oven brought to temperature and then turned off.

- After rising, bring the oven temperature to 350°F (static) or 325°F (convection) and bake the buns for 10–15 minutes. If you can wait to eat them, let them cool slightly, then whisk together icing ingredients, adding only enough milk to make a drizzling consistency, and pour over buns before serving.

MAKES 8–10 BUNS

Cinnamon Sticky Rolls

These are just like Grandma used to make. A word of warning though: get your roll first, or there might not be any left for you! My grandmother used to make two recipes of these rolls for our family gatherings: one with nuts and one without. She labeled them "male" and "female" rolls . . . think about it.

DOUGH:

2 cups Jules Gluten Free All Purpose Flour (pages 6, 8)

¼ cup milk powder (dairy or nondairy)

½ teaspoon baking soda

2 teaspoons baking powder, gluten-free

¼ cup shortening

3 tablespoons honey or agave nectar

2 large eggs or egg substitute of choice (like Egg Substitute #1 or 7, pages 15, 16)

²/3 cup vanilla yogurt (dairy or nondairy)

1 teaspoon apple cider vinegar

2¼ teaspoons (1 packet) rapid rise yeast, gluten-free

TOPPING:

4 tablespoons melted butter or nondairy alternative

½ cup dark Karo syrup or pure maple syrup

⅓ cup brown sugar

1 cup pecans, chopped (optional; omit if making nut-free)

CRUMBLE:

¼ cup butter or nondairy alternative, melted

1 cup brown sugar

1 tablespoon cinnamon

▸ In a large bowl, whisk together the dry ingredients, except yeast. Cut the shortening into small pieces and cut into the dry ingredients with a dough paddle attachment on an electric mixer or a pastry cutter by hand.

▸ In a smaller bowl, stir together the wet ingredients until combined. Slowly add liquid mixture to the dry ingredient bowl and mix with the paddle attachment. Add in the yeast, mixing on medium-high until smooth. Beat an additional 1–2 minutes thereafter. The dough will be very wet.

▸ Meanwhile, combine the topping ingredients and distribute in the bottom of an oiled 8 x 8-inch or 9-inch round pan.

▸ Preheat the oven to 200°F then turn off.

continues

- Liberally dust a clean counter or pastry mat and your hands with gluten-free flour or cornstarch. Turn the dough out onto the well-floured surface and gently pat into a rectangle shape, about ¼-inch thick, the longer side of the rectangle lying from 9 o'clock to 3 o'clock on a dial; the shorter side lying from 12 o'clock to 6 o'clock. The dough will be very sticky until coated with flour.

- In a small bowl mix together the crumble ingredients: melted butter, brown sugar, and cinnamon. Crumble this mixture on top of the dough, leaving ½ inch of the dough exposed at 12 o'clock and 6 o'clock on the rectangle. Cut the dough in half, from 12 o'clock to 6 o'clock on the rectangle, then slowly roll the dough up from 6 o'clock to 12 o'clock on each half of the cut rectangle, so that the crumble mixture is spiraled inside itself. There will now be two long logs of rolled dough. Slice each log with a knife to form 8–12 rolls. Place the rolls cut sides down in the pan so that they cover the topping. Cover the pan with a damp towel or sheet of wax paper sprayed with cooking oil and place inside the warmed oven for 25 minutes to rise.

- After rising, remove the towel and cover the pan with oiled aluminum foil. Raise the temperature in the oven to 350°F (static) or 325°F (convection).

- When the oven has come to temperature, return the covered pan to bake for approximately 25 minutes (remove the foil after 20 minutes). The rolls will be light brown and have risen nicely. If the rolls seem too wet at this point, recover with aluminum foil and bake another 5 minutes and test again.

- Repeat this process at five-minute intervals for up to 15 more minutes, if necessary. When the rolls have firmed up in the middle, so that they begin to hold their shape, turn the oven off and open the oven door to let the rolls cool slowly for about 5 minutes. Remove the pan from the oven and turn it upside down on a plate to cool for another 5 minutes. The rolls will drop onto the plate and the pan can be removed.

- Serve warm, but be sure to grab a roll for yourself before they're all gone!

MAKES 8–12 ROLLS, DEPENDING ON HOW SMALL YOU CUT THEM

Coffee Cake

I tend to think any cake is fair game for breakfast, but, if you're more traditional, you'll love this crumb-topped classic. Time it just right so you can serve and eat it warm, and your day will be off to a fabulous start—guaranteed.

CAKE:

1 ripe banana

½ cup black coffee, prepared

½ cup packed light brown sugar

½ cup butter or nondairy alternative, softened

2 large eggs or egg substitute of choice (like Ener-G Egg Replacer or Egg Substitute #1, 2, 3, or 4, page 15)

2 teaspoons vanilla extract, gluten-free

2 teaspoons pumpkin pie spice

2 cups Jules Gluten Free All Purpose Flour (pages 6, 8)

¼ cup mesquite flour (or Jules Gluten Free All Purpose Flour)

2 teaspoons baking powder, gluten-free

½ teaspoon baking soda

STREUSEL TOPPING (DOUBLE IF YOU REALLY LIKE YOUR STREUSEL!):

2 tablespoons butter or nondairy alternative, softened

2 tablespoons light brown sugar

½ teaspoon cinnamon

▸ Preheat the oven to 350°F (static) or 325°F (convection). Oil or spray an 8 x 8-inch baking pan.

▸ Mash the banana in a medium-size bowl. Pour coffee over the banana and set aside. Beat the sugar and butter together in a large bowl until light and fluffy. Add the eggs and vanilla and combine well. Mix in the mashed banana and coffee then gradually stir in the remaining dry ingredients, mixing until thoroughly combined.

▸ Pour the batter into the prepared pan and set aside.

▸ In a small bowl, stir together the topping ingredients with a fork. Crumble over the cake, then cut through the topping with a butter knife in a crisscross fashion lengthwise, then crossways, feathering the topping in the top of the batter.

▸ Bake for 40–45 minutes, or until the edges are lightly crisp and a cake tester inserted in the middle comes out clean.

SERVES 6–8

Cranberry Walnut Muffins

The tartness of cranberries marries the walnuts so well in this great muffin. But even without the nuts, the muffins are beautiful, moist, and sure to please.

½ cup butter or nondairy alternative

½ cup granulated cane sugar

2 large eggs or egg substitute of choice (like Ener-G Egg Replacer or Egg Substitute #1, 2, 4, 5, or 7, pages 15—16)

1 teaspoon vanilla extract, gluten-free

½ cup sour cream (dairy or nondairy) or coconut yogurt

1 ripe banana, mashed

1½ cups Jules Gluten Free All Purpose Flour (pages 6, 8)

2 tablespoons flaxseed meal (optional)

1 teaspoon baking soda

2 teaspoons baking powder, gluten-free

2 teaspoons cinnamon

3 cups fresh or frozen cranberries, chopped

½ cup walnuts, chopped (omit if making nut-free)

▸ Preheat the oven to 350°F (static) or 325°F (convection). Oil or line muffin tins with muffin papers and set aside.

▸ Cream the butter and sugar until the mixture is light and fluffy. Add the eggs and vanilla and beat well. Mix in the sour cream and banana until well blended.

▸ In a separate bowl, whisk together all the dry ingredients, then gradually incorporate them into the wet batter. Lastly, stir the cranberries and walnuts into the batter gently.

▸ Spoon the batter into the prepared muffin tins and bake for 25–30 minutes, or until the tops are lightly browned and they spring back to the touch.

▸ Cool for 10 minutes before removing from the muffin tins.

MAKES 21–23 MUFFINS

Danish Pastry

This flexible pastry dough can be filled with nearly anything you can imagine. I've gotten you started with the traditional cream cheese filling (with dairy-free option), as well as a yummy cinnamon-apple filling, but don't let that stop your breakfast creativity!

PASTRY DOUGH:

2 cups Jules Gluten Free All Purpose Flour (pages 6, 8)

3 tablespoons flaxseed meal (optional, but recommended)

½ teaspoon baking soda

2 teaspoons baking powder, gluten-free

¼ cup shortening

1 teaspoon apple cider vinegar

3 tablespoons honey or light agave nectar

2 eggs or egg substitute of choice (like Egg Substitute #1, 2, or 7, pages 15–16)

1 cup vanilla yogurt (dairy or nondairy)

2¼ teaspoons (1 packet) rapid rise yeast, gluten-free

EGG OR MILK WASH:

1 egg, mixed (do not use egg substitute) or ¼–½ cup milk (dairy or nondairy)

Cinnamon-sugar mixture or coarse sugar to sprinkle on tops of pastries before baking

▸ In a large bowl, whisk together the dry ingredients, except the yeast. Cut the shortening into small pieces and cut into the dry ingredients with a dough paddle attachment on an electric mixer or by hand using a pastry cutter.

▸ In a smaller bowl, stir together the liquid ingredients until combined. Slowly add the liquid mixture to the dry ingredient bowl, mixing with the paddle attachment until incorporated. Pour in the yeast, stirring until the lumps are removed from the dough. Beat an additional 1–2 minutes thereafter.

▸ Dust a clean counter or pastry mat and your hands with gluten-free flour or cornstarch. Grab 7 small fistfuls of wet dough, patting each into a 5-inch square. Lay the squares onto a baking sheet lined with parchment paper. Using a pastry brush, lightly brush off any excess flour.

MAKES APPROXIMATELY 7 DANISH SQUARES

continues

Cinnamon-Apple Filling

2 tablespoons butter or nondairy alternative

¼ cup light brown sugar

1 tablespoon cinnamon

3 firm fresh apples (e.g., Fuji, Gala, Honeycrisp, Pink Lady, Jonathan, or
Winesap), peeled and coarsely chopped

▸ Melt the butter in a skillet over medium heat. Add the brown sugar and cinnamon, stirring to combine. Add the apples and stir to coat with the butter mixture. Stir periodically to coat and keep cooking all the apples. Cook for 15–20 minutes, or until the butter mixture is thin and the apples are tender. Set aside to cool.

Cream Cheese Filling

12 ounces cream cheese (dairy or nondairy)

¾ cup granulated cane sugar

1 egg yolk or egg yolk substitute of choice (page 17)

1 teaspoon vanilla extract, gluten-free

▸ Whisk together the cream cheese, sugar, egg yolk, and vanilla until there are no lumps. Place in a sealed container and refrigerate or freeze until thickened.

continues

PASTRY METHODS:

Pinwheels:

▸ Using a pizza cutter or pastry wheel, cut a slit from each of the 4 corners almost to the center, but not intersecting or cutting through the center.

▸ Place a dollop of cream cheese filling or cinnamon-apple filling in the center.

▸ Fold every other tip into the center, and dab each corner with milk or water to help them to adhere to one another. Brush the exposed pastry with egg or milk wash and sprinkle with cinnamon-sugar mixture or coarse sugar. Repeat for remaining pastry squares.

▸ Cover the baking sheet with oiled wax paper and place in a warming drawer or oven preheated to 200°F then turned off for 30 minutes to rise.

▸ Preheat the oven to 350°F (static) or 325°F (convection). Remove the wax paper and bake for approximately 15 minutes, or until lightly browned and resistant to a light touch (i.e., when pressed with a gentle fingertip, it rebounds rather than leaving a divot).

Envelopes:

▸ Place a dollop of cream cheese filling or cinnamon-apple filling in the center of each square and brush the remaining exposed pastry with egg or milk wash.

▸ Fold each opposite corner into the center, and dab each corner with milk or water to help them to adhere to one another. Once finished with each of the pastries, brush the entire exposed pastry with egg or milk wash, sprinkle with cinnamon-sugar mixture or coarse sugar, and cover the baking sheet with oiled wax paper. Place in a warming drawer or oven preheated to 200°F then turned off for 30 minutes to rise.

▸ Preheat the oven to 350°F (static) or 325°F (convection). Remove the wax paper and bake for approximately 15 minutes, or until lightly browned and resistant to a light touch (i.e., when pressed with a gentle fingertip, it rebounds rather than leaving a divot).

Blanket:

▸ Turn the square so that it is now a diamond shape with a tip at the top and the bottom. Place an elongated dollop of cream cheese filling or cinnamon-apple filling in the center and extend to the top and bottom corners, leaving the right and left corners without filling, and brush the remaining exposed pastry with egg or milk wash.

▸ Fold the right and left corners into the center, and dab each corner with milk or water to help them to adhere to one another.

continues

▸ Once finished with each of the pastries, brush the entire exposed pastry with egg or milk wash, sprinkle with cinnamon-sugar mixture or coarse sugar, and cover the baking sheet with oiled wax paper. Place in a warming drawer or oven preheated to 200°F then turned off for 30 minutes to rise.

▸ Preheat the oven to 350°F (static) or 325°F (convection). Remove the wax paper and bake for approximately 15 minutes, or until lightly browned and resistant to a light touch (i.e., when pressed with a gentle fingertip, it rebounds rather than leaving a divot).

English Muffins

I skip the step of frying this bread before serving, and no one has ever complained! This expedited version is deliciously crispy on the outside and moist and airy on the inside and perhaps best of all, healthier and simpler to make.

1 tablespoon rapid rise yeast, gluten-free

1 teaspoon granulated cane sugar

1¼ cups warm water

3 cups Jules Gluten Free All Purpose Flour (pages 6, 8)

½ teaspoon sea salt

½ teaspoon baking powder, gluten-free

3 tablespoons granulated cane sugar

3 large egg whites or egg white substitute (like 1½ recipes of Egg Substitute #1 or 7, pages 15–16)

4 tablespoons canola oil

▸ Combine the yeast, 1 teaspoon sugar, and warm water together, stir, and set aside.

▸ Whisk together dry the ingredients (flour, salt, and baking powder) and set aside.

▸ In a large bowl, combine the 3 tablespoons of sugar, egg whites, and oil. Whisk together, then add the yeast mixture. Beat with an electric mixer and slowly add the flour mixture, beating for 2–3 minutes after mixed to make the dough more airy.

▸ Oil or butter popover tins, jumbo muffin tins, bun trays, or English Muffin rings laid on a parchment-lined baking sheet, then spoon the dough into the trays, filling about two-thirds full. Cover with oiled wax paper and set aside to rise for 30 minutes in a warming drawer or oven preheated to 200°F then turned off.

▸ Once risen, bake at 350°F (static) or 325°F (convection) for 20 minutes, or until the muffins are cooked through and are light brown. If baking in popover or muffin tins, slice each muffin twice, to yield three English Muffins per tin.

MAKES 15–18 SLICED MUFFINS

Fresh Fruit Bread

I don't know about you, but I am a sucker for fresh fruit. In fact, my kitchen is notoriously so full of fruit that there seems to always be something getting ready to turn before I can use it all up! So it happened one day that I found I had both bananas and pears that were begging to be used. I tried to think creatively of a recipe other than cobbler or crumble that might successfully incorporate both ingredients. I ultimately devised a quick bread loaf that can easily be made dairy-free and that has now won a place in my heart. This recipe is light, moist, flavorful, and addictive! Feel free to change up the fruits according to what is in your kitchen, but be sure to add extra sugar if you are using tart fruits like cranberries.

1½ cups Jules Gluten Free All Purpose Flour (pages 6, 8)
¾ cup granulated cane sugar
½ teaspoon baking soda
2 teaspoons baking powder, gluten-free
1 teaspoon cinnamon
2 large eggs or egg substitute of choice (like Ener-G Egg Replacer or
    Egg Substitute #1, 2, 5, or 7, pages 15–16)
¼ cup vanilla yogurt (dairy or nondairy)
1 teaspoon vanilla extract, gluten-free
1 medium-size ripe banana, mashed
1 very ripe pear or apple, peeled and chopped
¼ cup baking raisins (or boil raisins in water, drain, then add to the recipe)
½ cup pecans, chopped (optional; omit if making nut-free)

▸ Preheat the oven to 350°F (static) or 325°F (convection).

▸ Butter or oil a loaf pan and lightly sprinkle with gluten-free flour until coated.

▸ Whisk the dry ingredients in a large mixing bowl. Mix the egg, yogurt, and vanilla together, then add the dry ingredients. Fold in the mashed banana, fresh fruit, raisins, and pecans.

▸ Pour the batter into the prepared pan and bake for 45–50 minutes, or until a cake tester inserted into the center comes out clean. Remove to a wire rack and slice when cooled.

MAKES 1 LOAF

Fruity Snack Bars

Feel free to substitute dried fruits and/or nuts you may have on hand—the base recipe remains the same—although I recommend at least using figs in this recipe, as they are high in fiber and minerals like potassium, calcium, and iron, and their crunchy sweetness is unmistakable throughout.

Be sure to let the bars cool before you cut them, and if you have any extra crumbs left behind from cutting the bars, save them to sprinkle on top of yogurt or use as a granola-like breakfast cereal with milk. Any way you prefer, these nutritious gluten- and dairy-free bars are sure to be a hit!

1 cup butter or nondairy alternative, room temperature
¾ cup light brown sugar
⅓ cup granulated cane sugar
2 teaspoons vanilla extract, gluten-free
½ teaspoon almond extract, gluten-free (omit if making tree nut–free)
2 large eggs or egg substitute of choice (like Egg Substitute #1, 2, 4, 5, 6, or 7, pages 15–16)
2 cups Jules Gluten Free All Purpose Flour (pages 6, 8)
¾ teaspoon baking soda
1 teaspoon ground cinnamon
½ teaspoon salt
1 cup pecans or walnuts, chopped (if making nut-free, omit or substitute with seeds)
1 cup dried tart cherries or cranberries
1 cup dried figs, chopped
½ cup golden raisins or dried blueberries
½ cup dried dates, apricots, or other dried fruit, chopped

continues

▸ Preheat the oven to 350°F. Prepare a jelly roll pan (approximately 15 x 10-inch) or cookie sheet with raised edges by wrapping foil over the top of the pan and greasing the foil-wrapped pan with cooking spray, shortening, or butter. Set aside.

▸ In a large mixing bowl, cream the butter with the sugars, beating until the dough is light and fluffy. Gradually add in the vanilla, almond extract, and eggs.

▸ In a separate bowl, whisk together the gluten-free flour, baking soda, cinnamon, and salt. Slowly beat this dry mixture into the first large bowl, mixing until incorporated.

▸ Chop the nuts and dried fruit and stir into the dough. Spread the thick dough evenly across the prepared pan and bake for approximately 25 minutes, or until lightly browned on top and a toothpick inserted into the center comes out clean.

▸ Cool fully before cutting or removing. Cut horizontally and vertically (like a window pane) to form brownie-size bars and remove carefully to a plate.

SERVES 10

Granola

Even if you can't have nuts, don't let their absence stop you from making a big ol' batch of this healthy recipe, just get creative with seed substitutions like toasted pepitas (pumpkin seeds) and add teff as another crunchy, nutritious ingredient. Many granola recipes have oil in their liquid ingredients (and the accompanying fat). Not so this one. Make this granola your own: triple the cinnamon if you like, double the vanilla or omit it altogether . . . you get the picture. Serve this with your favorite milk or yogurt, or on salads, and take it along when you travel. This will become a staple for your family, as it has with mine. To your health!

DRY

6 cups certified gluten-free oats, quinoa flakes, or rice flakes
1 cup pine nuts or ½ cup pepitas (pumpkin seeds), roasted
1 cup sunflower seeds
1 cup flaxseed meal
1 cup quinoa flakes, rice bran, or certified gluten-free oat bran
1 cup coconut, grated
½ cup pecans, finely chopped (omit if making nut-free)
½ cup walnuts, finely chopped (omit if making nut-free)
2–3 cups baking raisins or dried cranberries, to taste
Dash of salt
1–3 tablespoons (yes, tablespoons) cinnamon, to taste
Dash of allspice

LIQUID

1 cup pure maple syrup or dark agave nectar
1 teaspoon vanilla extract, gluten-free
⅜ cup honey or light agave nectar
⅜ cup molasses (e.g., blackstrap molasses)

continues

- Preheat the oven to 325°F.

- Mix the dry ingredients well in a large bowl.

- Over low heat, warm all of the liquid ingredients in a saucepan; pour warmed liquid over the dry mix and combine thoroughly.

- Spread evenly over two large lightly oiled or parchment-lined cookie sheets.

- Bake for 25 minutes. Turn off the oven and remove the cookie sheets. Stir, loosen, and re-distribute the granola on the cookie sheets with a wooden spoon or spatula. Return the sheets to the still-warm oven for at least 5 minutes, or until desired crunchiness is achieved.

- When cooled, seal in airtight containers.

MAKES 15 CUPS

Granola Bars

I'd recommend doubling this recipe right off the bat. Portable, hearty, healthy, soft, and chewy . . . you're going to love it, and probably end up sharing the bars, packing them in lunches, and stowing some in your car. Actually, maybe you should triple the recipe!

¼ cup flaxseed meal

1 cup Jules Gluten Free All Purpose Flour (pages 6, 8) or certified gluten-free oat flour

3 cups certified gluten-free rolled oats, rice flakes, or quinoa flakes

1 tablespoon cinnamon

½ cup dried apples, chopped

½ cup dried bananas, chopped

¼ cup dates, chopped

¾ cup baking raisins (or boil raisins in water, drain, then add to the recipe)

1 cup walnuts, chopped (if making nut-free, omit)

½ cup figs, chopped

½ cup agave nectar, honey, or maple syrup

1 cup unsweetened applesauce

¼ cup sunflower "nut" butter (if making nut-free) or "natural" peanut, almond, or cashew butter

¾ cup unsweetened apple juice or cider

▸ Preheat the oven to 375°F.

▸ Line a jelly roll baking pan with aluminum foil and spray with cooking oil.

▸ In a large mixing bowl, stir together the flaxseed meal, gluten-free flour, oats, cinnamon, and fruits and nuts of your choice (in similar proportions to those listed above). When fully combined, stir in the agave nectar, applesauce, nut butter, and juice, mixing with a large wooden spoon until totally incorporated. The mixture should be wet enough to press together for baking.

▸ Pack the mixture into the bottom of the prepared baking pan and press down with the back of a rubber spatula or large wooden spoon. Bake for 30 minutes or until the edges begin to brown slightly.

▸ Remove from the oven and cut into bars before cooled. Once fully cooled, remove from the pan by lifting the foil edges out and gently removing all the bars while still on top of the foil.

MAKES APPROXIMATELY 20 BARS

Lemon Poppyseed Muffins

These little gems are so unique, the lemon gives them such a fresh, light flavor and the poppyseeds add visual interest as well. I often sample these at shows and at my cooking classes . . . and they've elicited so many recipe requests that I had to print up recipe cards to accompany them.

MUFFINS:

2 cups Jules Gluten Free All Purpose Flour (pages 6, 8)

1 teaspoon baking soda

¼ teaspoon baking powder, gluten-free

¼ teaspoon sea salt

2 teaspoons lemon or orange rind, grated finely

⅛ cup poppy seeds

⅓ cup butter or nondairy alternative

½ cup granulated cane sugar

2 large eggs or egg substitute of choice (like Ener-G Egg Replacer or Egg Substitute #1, 2, 6, or 7, pages 15–16)

½ cup vanilla yogurt (dairy or nondairy)

¼ cup lemon juice

½ teaspoon almond extract, gluten-free (omit if avoiding nuts)

¼ cup vanilla nondairy milk (or you may use cow's milk plus ½ teaspoon vanilla extract, gluten-free)

GLAZE (OPTIONAL):

⅓ cup confectioner's sugar

2 tablespoons lemon juice

½ teaspoon vanilla extract, gluten-free

¼ teaspoon almond extract, gluten-free (omit if avoiding nuts)

continues

▸ Preheat the oven to 375°F (static) or 350°F (convection).

▸ Whisk the dry ingredients together and set aside.

▸ In a large mixing bowl, cream the butter and sugar together until light and fluffy. Mix in the eggs and beat until incorporated. Stir in the remaining liquid ingredients (yogurt, lemon juice, almond extract, and milk). Once combined, gradually add in the dry ingredients, beating until the batter is smooth.

▸ Scoop equal portions of the batter into oiled or lined muffin tins and bake for 20–22 minutes. The muffins should be slightly golden on top and have nice crowns.

▸ Remove from the oven and cool in the muffin tin for 5 minutes, then go around the inside of each muffin cup with a knife to gently loosen the muffin. Place each muffin on a cooling rack to cool until ready to glaze or serve.

▸ To make the glaze, stir together the glaze ingredients until smooth. If the mixture is too thick, add milk by the teaspoon (dairy or nondairy); if it is too thin, add additional confectioner's sugar by the teaspoon. Drizzle the glaze in a crisscross pattern across the top of each muffin before serving.

MAKES 12 MUFFINS

Multigrain Confetti Muffins

These muffins are aptly named, as they include a host of alternative gluten-free grains and flours and when broken open, look like a big New Year's party! If you don't happen to have any of these grains on hand, simply use the same measurement of Jules Gluten Free All Purpose Flour.

½ cup chai tea latte (prepare or brew according to package directions)

½ cup certified gluten-free oats

4 tablespoons butter or nondairy alternative

⅓ cup granulated cane sugar

2 tablespoons honey or agave nectar

½ cup natural applesauce, apple butter, or pumpkin butter

2 large eggs or egg substitute of choice (like Ener-G Egg Replacer or Egg Substitute #1, 2, 3, 4, or 7, pages 15–16)

1 cup Jules Gluten Free All Purpose Flour (pages 6, 8)

½ cup almond meal, brown rice flour, buckwheat flour, or Jules Gluten Free All Purpose Flour

2 tablespoons flaxseed meal

2 tablespoons mesquite flour or Jules Gluten Free All Purpose Flour

2 teaspoons baking powder, gluten-free

½ teaspoon baking soda

1 teaspoon ground cinnamon

1½ cups fresh or frozen berries, chopped (cranberries, blueberries, etc.)

1 cup walnuts, chopped (optional; omit if making nut-free)

▸ Preheat the oven to 350°F (static) or 325°F (convection, preferred).

▸ Coat the muffin tins with cooking oil or line with muffin papers.

▸ In a small glass bowl (for microwave) or a small saucepan (for stovetop), combine the prepared chai tea with the oats and boil for 2 minutes, stir, cover, and set aside.

▸ In a large mixing bowl, cream the butter with the sugar. Beat in the agave nectar, applesauce, eggs, and finally, the cooked oat mixture. Gradually stir in the remaining dry ingredients and mix until smooth. Lastly, fold in the chopped berries and walnuts, if using.

▸ Fill the muffin tins two-thirds full and bake until they are light brown, approximately 22 minutes for regular-size muffins. Remove from the oven to cool in the pan.

MAKES APPROXIMATELY 15 MUFFINS

Nut Butter Muffins

These fun muffins have a great, subtle taste. Whether you use peanut butter or sunflower "nut" butter, they're just begging for a big dollop of jelly . . . PB&J for breakfast!

½ cup creamy peanut butter or nut-free "nut" butter
(soy "nut" butter or sunflower "nut" butter)

2 tablespoons butter or nondairy alternative, room temperature

⅔ cup light brown sugar, packed, or ⅓ cup agave nectar plus
3 tablespoons molasses

2 eggs plus 1 egg white (do not add egg white if using agave and
molasses substitute) or egg substitute of choice (like 2½ recipes of
Ener-G Egg Replacer or Egg Substitute #1, 2, 3, 4, 6, or 7, pages 15–16)

1 teaspoon vanilla extract, gluten-free

1 cup Jules Gluten Free All Purpose Flour (pages 6, 8)

1 teaspoon baking powder, gluten-free

4 tablespoons milk (dairy or nondairy)

½ cup baking raisins or chocolate chips
(gluten-, dairy-, and soy-free brands include Sunspire and Enjoy Life)

▸ Preheat the oven to 350°F (static) or 325°F (convection).

▸ Line with muffin papers or oil 12 muffin tins.

▸ Measure nut butter, butter, and brown sugar (or agave and molasses) into a large mixing bowl. Beat together with a dough paddle rather than a whisk attachment on your mixer. If you do not have a dough paddle, you can stir with a wooden spoon until well mixed. Beat in the eggs, mixing well after each addition. Add the vanilla last.

▸ Stir together the dry ingredients then add them to the mixing bowl. Pour in the milk and stir slowly until thoroughly mixed. Add the raisins or chocolate chips and spoon into the muffin tins, filling only about one-third to one-half full.

▸ Bake for 15–20 minutes, or until light brown crowns have formed and they are springy to the touch. Let cool for at least 5 minutes before removing.

MAKES 12 MUFFINS

Pancakes

My kids love pancakes. They've had them so often, they're quite literally connoisseurs. These cook up thicker, yet light and fluffy with crispy edges. They passed the test and I think it is officially our new favorite pancake recipe. I hope your family enjoys them one morning very soon!

1½ cups Jules Gluten Free All Purpose Flour (pages 6, 8)

4 tablespoons DariFree Non-Dairy Milk Powder (or dairy or soy milk powder)

1 tablespoon granulated cane sugar

1½ teaspoons gluten-free baking powder

½ teaspoon baking soda

½ teaspoon salt

2 eggs or egg substitute of choice (like Egg Substitute #1, 4, 5, 6, or 7, pages 15–16)

3 tablespoons canola oil

Approximately 1½ cups milk (dairy or nondairy vanilla milk)

Canola oil or other high-heat oil for the pan

Berries, if desired

▸ Pour enough oil into a large skillet or griddle to have a thin covering over the entire surface. Heat the skillet or griddle to medium-high.

▸ In a medium bowl, whisk together the dry ingredients and set aside. In another larger bowl, combine all the liquid ingredients, using only 1¼ cups of milk at first. Gradually whisk the dry ingredients into the liquid ingredient bowl until well mixed and only a few lumps remain. Add more milk as needed to thin the batter to the point that it is easily spooned onto the skillet, but is not watery at all. You should be able to put a dollop of batter onto the hot oil and spread the batter out with the back of a spoon to form a circle without the batter being too thick or too runny.

▸ Spoon the batter onto the skillet and spread the batter with the back of a large spoon. Leave space between each pancake so that you can use a spatula to flip each one easily. If desired, place fresh or frozen berries onto the uncooked side of the pancakes in a design (like a Mickey Mouse face) or randomly.

▸ Cook until bubbles begin to form in the batter, then gently flip, continuing to cook until light brown on the bottom with slightly crispy edges.

▸ Serve warm with maple syrup, or once cooled, layer with pieces of wax paper between the pancakes, and seal in a zip-top bag; refrigerate or freeze and reheat for later serving.

SERVES 6

See photo insert.

Pop-Tarts

Thought you'd had your last Pop-Tart? Think again! Not only are these delicious (the most important thing, right?!), but they are easy (another bonus!). To make this recipe even easier, simply use my Jules Gluten Free Graham Cracker/Gingersnap Mix (available from www.JulesGlutenFree.com) and follow the directions below.

PASTRY DOUGH:

¾ cup shortening, butter, or nondairy alternative
1 cup light brown sugar or Brown Sugar Splenda
¼ cup honey or agave nectar
1 teaspoon vanilla extract, gluten-free
1½ cups Jules Gluten Free All Purpose Flour (pages 6, 8)
1 cup fine white rice flour
½ cup buckwheat or brown rice flour
Dash of salt
2 teaspoons cinnamon
3 teaspoons baking powder, gluten-free
Approximately ½ cup water

FILLING:

Jam, jelly, quince paste, or your favorite filling

▸ Cream the shortening, brown sugar, honey, and vanilla until light and fluffy. Stir in the remaining dry ingredients, then slowly stir in enough water to form a ball of dough that holds together nicely but is not so wet that it is sticky. Scoop dough into a smaller container and cover tightly. Place it in the refrigerator overnight or freeze for 2 hours until very cold.

▸ Preheat the oven to 325°F (static) or 300°F (convection).

▸ Line cookie sheets with parchment paper and set aside.

continues

▸ Prepare a clean counter surface or pastry mat by dusting with gluten-free flour. Coat a rolling pin as well. Scoop half of the dough out onto the mat and roll to the thickness of a graham cracker (⅛–¼-inch thick). Using a clean knife or a pastry wheel, cut out equal-size rectangles, the size of a normal toaster pastry (approximately 3 x 4½ inches).

▸ Gently lift one rectangle onto the parchment paper with a spatula. Scoop out jam, jelly, quince paste, or your favorite filling into the middle and spread a thick layer, leaving at least ¼ inch all around to seal the pastry. Wet your fingers and go around the perimeter of the pastry (the part with no filling) and the perimeter of another rectangle, which you will be placing on top. Lift the other rectangle and place it directly on top of the rectangle with the filling. Gently go around the perimeter of the sealed pastry with the tines of a fork and press the edges of the two rectangles together, making a design impress with the fork tines. Repeat with all the other rectangles, and when your cookie sheets are filled, bake for 25–30 minutes, or until lightly browned.

MAKES 12 TOASTER PASTRIES

GLAZE (OPTIONAL):

1 cup sifted confectioner's sugar

½ teaspoon vanilla extract, gluten-free (you may use orange, almond, or other extract as an alternative)

2–4 teaspoons milk (dairy or nondairy) or fruit juice

▸ Whisk together the sugar, vanilla extract, and milk by gradually adding the milk, a teaspoon or so at a time. Continue adding the milk until the frosting is the consistency you need to be able to drizzle over the pastry without it running off the top. Drizzle in lines or spoon on top of the pastry once cooled. Allow it to sit until the glaze is set before serving.

Pumpkin-Banana Bread

You can play with the pumpkin-to-banana proportions in this easy recipe to dial in just the right amount of either to suit your family's tastes. When canned pumpkin is available, this will be one of your go-to recipes!

2 large eggs or egg substitute of choice (like Ener-G Egg Replacer or Egg Substitute #1, 3, 4, or 7, pages 15–16)
¼ cup canola oil
2 ripe bananas, mashed
1⅓ cups pumpkin puree
¼ cup granulated cane sugar
¼ cup brown sugar
Scant ½ cup honey or agave nectar
2½ cups Jules Gluten Free All Purpose Flour (pages 6, 8)
2 teaspoons baking powder, gluten-free
½ teaspoon baking soda
Pinch of salt
1 tablespoon pumpkin pie spice
¼ cup dried cranberries (optional)
¼ cup pecans or walnuts, chopped (optional; omit if making nut-free)

▸ Preheat the oven to 350°F (static) or 325°F (convection).

▸ Combine the eggs, oil, banana, pumpkin, sugars, and honey. Mix on medium speed until the granulated sugars are well blended and the batter turns a lighter color and consistency. Stir in the dry ingredients until well mixed, then add the cranberries and nuts, if desired.

▸ Pour into a greased 9 x 5-inch loaf pan, 4 small loaf pans, or lined muffin tins.

▸ Bake for approximately 45 minutes for the large loaf, 25–30 minutes for the smaller pans, 20–25 minutes for the muffins, and 15 minutes or so for the mini-muffins. Insert a cake tester into the center of the bread to determine when done. Cool the loaves in the pans for at least 10 minutes before removing from the pans to fully cool.

**MAKES 1 LOAF, 4 SMALL LOAVES,
15 REGULAR-SIZE MUFFINS, OR 24 MINI-MUFFINS**

Pumpkin Corn Muffins

An autumnal twist to cornbread. A faint orange hue, a distinctive pumpkin taste, and many happy returns to this easy recipe, for sure.

1 large egg or egg substitute of choice (like Ener-G Egg Replacer or Egg Substitute #1, 2, 3, or 4, page 15)

1 cup milk (dairy or nondairy)

½ teaspoon apple cider vinegar

⅔ cup pumpkin puree

1 cup Jules Gluten Free All Purpose Flour (pages 6, 8)

½ teaspoon salt

½ teaspoon baking soda

1 tablespoon baking powder, gluten-free

¾ cup cornmeal

½ cup granulated cane sugar

1 teaspoon pumpkin pie spice

2 tablespoons flaxseed meal (optional)

▸ Preheat the oven to 350°F (static) or 325°F (convection).

▸ Mix the liquid ingredients including pumpkin until combined. Whisk in the dry ingredients until the lumps are removed. Expect the batter to be a bit thin, but not watery.

▸ Pour the batter into an oiled 8 x 8-inch baking pan or into oiled or lined muffin tins. Bake for 30 minutes for the cornbread, 20 minutes for regular corn muffins, or 12–15 minutes for mini-muffins. Insert a cake tester into the center of the bread to test for doneness.

MAKES APPROXIMATELY 18 REGULAR-SIZE MUFFINS, 40 MINI-MUFFINS, OR ONE 8-INCH SQUARE PAN OF CORNBREAD SQUARES

Pumpkin Pancakes

You know, why not? Pumpkin's so good, you just *have* to try it in . . . well . . . pancakes! Pumpkin's healthy for you, so add it to breakfast in pancake form. Add some strategically placed chocolate chips after flipping, and make some jack-o-lanterns while you're at it.

1¼ cups Jules Gluten Free All Purpose Flour (pages 6, 8)

1½ teaspoons baking powder, gluten-free

1 teaspoon pumpkin pie spice

1 teaspoon cinnamon

1 large egg or egg substitute of choice (like Egg Substitute #1, 3, 4, or 7, pages 15–16)

2 tablespoons canola oil

1 tablespoon brown sugar, packed

½ cup pureed pumpkin

1½ cups milk (dairy or nondairy)

½ cup raisins, cranberries or chocolate chips, dairy or nondairy (optional)

Canola oil or other high heat oil for the pan

▸ Sift the flour, baking powder, and spices together and set aside.

▸ Whisk the egg, oil, and brown sugar until mixed. Stir in the pumpkin, then add this wet mixture to the dry ingredients. Slowly add the milk while stirring, until blended. Fold in raisins other add-ins if using.

▸ Using an electric skillet or large skillet over medium-high heat, add enough oil to lightly coat the entire surface.

▸ Carefully add spoonfuls of the batter to the hot oil, spreading the batter with the back of a spoon to thin it out. Flip when the uncooked side begins to bubble and the cooking surface is golden brown.

▸ Serve warm with maple syrup or confectioner's sugar.

SERVES 4

Scones

Shake any preconceived notions you have about scones being dry. These are anything but! Moist, flavorful, and delicious with nearly any fruit, nut, or chip mixed in, they are versatile as well.

> 2 cups Jules Gluten Free All Purpose Flour (pages 6, 8)
> ¼ cup granulated cane sugar
> 2 teaspoons baking powder, gluten-free
> ½ teaspoon baking soda
> 4 tablespoons shortening, butter, or nondairy alternative
> 2 large eggs or egg substitute of choice (like Ener-G Egg Replacer or Egg Substitute #1 or 7, pages 15, 16)
> ¾ cup vanilla yogurt (dairy or nondairy)
> ½ cup fresh or frozen berries, raisins, orange rind, chopped nuts (omit if making nut-free), chocolate chips, etc.
> Cinnamon-sugar mixture to sprinkle on the tops before baking

▸ Preheat the oven to 400°F (static) or 375°F (convection, preferred).

▸ Whisk together all dry ingredients in a large-bottom bowl. Cut shortening or butter into the dry ingredients using a pastry cutter or two knives or simply combine in a food processor. Stir in the eggs and yogurt until well mixed.

▸ Add any berries, nuts, raisins, etc. Scoop heaping tablespoonfuls onto a parchment-lined baking sheet, sprinkle with the cinnamon-sugar mixture, and bake for 10–12 minutes, or until the tops are lightly browned and there are no uncooked portions peeking through. Do not overcook!

SERVES 6

Maple-Oat Scones

Make these tasty scones the next time you have company, and they'll think they're staying at a sophisticated bed & breakfast. You don't have to tell them these are simple to make. But do tell them that the addition of oats increases the fiber and adds a great taste. And the glaze? They'll book another night!

1¼ cups certified gluten-free rolled oats (or gluten-free oat flour)

2 cups Jules Gluten Free All Purpose Flour (pages 6, 8)

¼ cup granulated cane sugar

½ teaspoon baking soda

2 teaspoons baking powder, gluten-free

¼ cup shortening, butter, or nondairy alternative

2 large eggs or egg substitute of choice (like Ener-G Egg Replacer or Egg Substitute #1 or 7, pages 15, 16)

1 cup vanilla yogurt (dairy or nondairy)

2 tablespoons pure maple syrup (or dark agave nectar)

GLAZE (OPTIONAL):

1½ cups confectioner's sugar

2-plus tablespoons vanilla (dairy or nondairy) milk

2 tablespoons pure maple syrup (or dark agave nectar)

▸ Preheat the oven to 400°F (static) or 375°F (convection, preferred).

▸ Pour the oats into a blender or food processor and blend into a fine flour, or measure out 1¼ cups gluten-free oat flour.

▸ In a large bowl whisk together the dry oat flour, gluten-free flour, sugar, baking soda, and baking powder. Cut in the shortening or butter using a pastry cutter, two knives, or an electric mixer.

▸ In a small bowl, stir the eggs together with a fork to mix. Pour eggs into the mixed dry ingredients, then add the yogurt and maple syrup. Stir well to combine.

▸ Turn the dough onto a clean counter or pastry mat liberally dusted with gluten-free flour or cornstarch. Coat your hands with the flour as well, then scoop the dough in a ball onto the mat.

continues

▸ Pat the dough out into a flat rectangle, approximately 1-inch thick. Using a butter knife, cut the dough into three sections, then cut each section into smaller triangles. You should wind up with approximately 12 triangle-shaped scones. Make sure there is not too much extra flour on the tops of the scones before baking—brush off lightly with a pastry brush, if necessary.

▸ Place each scone onto a parchment-lined cookie sheet and bake for approximately 10 minutes, or until they spring back when lightly touched. Do not overcook! Remove the entire baking sheet to a wire rack to cool.

▸ After cooling for at least 5 minutes, stir together the glaze ingredients, adding the milk only one tablespoon at a time until it reaches a pourable, but not thin, glaze consistency. Slowly pour over the top of each scone. Some of the glaze will pool around the scones onto the parchment paper, so leave the scones on the baking sheet for this glaze step unless you are serving immediately and want the glaze to pool on the serving plates.

MAKES A BAKER'S DOZEN

Zucchini Bread

Traditional zucchini bread has always seemed unnaturally high in oil to me. In this recipe, I've opted against the traditional use of oil in the bread, as I found that it made the bread too, well, . . . oily! The taste is light, very moist, not too sweet, and definitely not oily.

A wonderful bread, especially served as a muffin or mini-muffin—share the love with all your friends. They'll want more, I promise!

½ cup granulated cane sugar

½ cup shortening, butter, or nondairy alternative

2 large eggs or egg substitute of choice (like Egg Substitute #1 or 6, pages 15, 16)

½ cup sour cream (dairy or nondairy) or coconut yogurt

1 teaspoon vanilla extract, gluten-free

½ cup mashed ripe banana (approximately 1 banana)

2 cups Jules Gluten Free All Purpose Flour (pages 6, 8)

2 tablespoons flaxseed meal (optional, but recommended)

1 tablespoon cinnamon

1 tablespoon baking powder, gluten-free

1 teaspoon baking soda

1 cup packed fresh zucchini, unpeeled and grated (approximately 1 zucchini squash)

½ cup chopped pecans or walnuts (optional; omit if making nut-free)

Cinnamon and sugar mixture to sprinkle on top

▸ Preheat the oven to 350°F (static) or 325°F (convection).

▸ Beat the sugar and shortening until fluffy, then add the eggs, vanilla, and mashed banana.

▸ Sift all the dry ingredients in a large mixing bowl. Pour slowly into the wet ingredient bowl and beat together until integrated. Fold in the zucchini and nuts. The batter will be stiff.

▸ If baking as mini-loaves, oil 5–6 small loaf pans, filling each no more than one-half full, and sprinkle with cinnamon-sugar mixture. Bake for approximately 35 minutes, testing to be sure the middle is cooked through. If baking as muffins, oil and fill 24 muffin tins halfway full and sprinkle with cinnamon-sugar mixture. Bake for approximately 30 minutes, testing to be sure the middle is cooked through.

MAKES 6 SMALL LOAVES OR 24 MUFFINS

2

Appetizers and Side Dishes

New Year's Cabbage

Greens like cabbage, collards, kale, and chard are often consumed around the world on New Year's Day because their cooked green leaves look so much like folded money—and who couldn't use some tasty economic good fortune?!

> 1 small head of cabbage, rinsed and chopped
> 3 tablespoons water
> ½ small onion, diced
> 2 tablespoons extra-virgin olive oil
> 2 tablespoons balsamic vinegar
> 1½ teaspoons granulated cane sugar
> Salt and pepper, to taste

▸ In a large skillet over medium heat, cook the cabbage and water with the lid on, stirring occasionally, until wilted.

▸ In a small bowl, stir together the remaining ingredients to form a thin sauce. Pour over the cooking cabbage and continue stirring until warm. Remove from the heat and serve immediately. May be reheated for serving later.

SERVES 6–8

Charoset

While this traditionally Jewish dish is associated with the Passover table, it is a lovely fruit salad in its own right and may also be served with crackers or Matzo (see page 89).

2 apples, peeled, cored, and cut into cubes
2 cups sliced almonds or chopped walnuts (substitute with equal parts coconut and pepitas/pumpkin seeds if avoiding nuts)
1 teaspoon cinnamon
½ cup freshly squeezed orange juice
1 tablespoon freshly squeezed lemon juice
¾ cup currants, dates, or baking raisins (or boil raisins, drain, and use)

▸ In a food processor, combine the apples, nuts, cinnamon, orange juice, lemon juice, and currants. Pulse briefly until the desired texture is achieved. Stir in the seeds and coconut, if using.

SERVES 4

Coconut Rice

Coconuts are prized around the world for their healing properties. Added to a dish like rice, nutritious coconut boosts its fiber, vitamins, and minerals, and freshly toasted coconut also adds an aromatic element that complements so many dishes.

> 1 cup light coconut milk
> 1 cup water
> Pinch of salt
> 1 cup brown rice
> ⅓ cup unsweetened fresh flaked coconut
> 2 tablespoons sweetened coconut

▸ Boil the liquids and salt in a large saucepan over high heat. Add the rice and return to a boil. Reduce to a low simmer and cover until the liquid is absorbed—cook time will differ depending on the grain (follow package directions).

▸ Meanwhile, toast the unsweetened coconut in an oven preheated to 300°F. Spread the coconut onto a baking sheet lined with aluminum foil and stir periodically while toasting to prevent burning. Toast for 20–30 minutes, until lightly browned.

▸ When the rice is finished cooking, remove it from the heat and let it sit, covered, until the coconut is toasted. Once toasted, add all the coconut to the rice, stir, and serve warm with grilled fish or chicken.

SERVES 4

Cornbread Stuffing

If you're from the South, like me, you may already have a near-and-dear corn-bread stuffing recipe. In that case, you'll just need to incorporate my Cornbread recipe (page 107) into your own. If cornbread stuffing is new to you, you owe it to yourself to give it a try! It's beautiful, smells divine, and after your family gets over the shock of having a "different" stuffing, they'll probably find themselves heaping their plates with a second helping. Enjoy!

1 recipe Cornbread (page 107)
2 tablespoons butter or nondairy alternative
½ cup diced celery
¾ cup diced sweet onion
2 cups vegetable stock, gluten-free
½ cup fresh or frozen cranberries, chopped (optional)
½ cup pecans, chopped (optional; omit if making nut-free)
1 teaspoon celery salt
¾ teaspoon cinnamon
⅛ teaspoon marjoram
2 teaspoons dried sage

▸ Preheat the oven to 300°F.

▸ Allow the cooked cornbread to cool, then cut the cornbread into ¾-inch cubes and spread onto a baking sheet. Bake the cornbread cubes for 30 minutes or more, until they are browned, lightly toasted, and dried out; toss periodically while toasting to crisp each cube all around.

▸ Raise the oven temperature to 350°F.

▸ Meanwhile, melt the butter in a large skillet over medium-high heat. Sauté the celery and onion until soft. Add the stock, toasted cornbread, cranberries, nuts (if using), and spices and herbs, mixing together well. Pour the stuffing into an oiled 9 x 11-inch baking dish and bake for 25–30 minutes.

▸ Serve warm.

SERVES 8

Cornmeal-Crusted Zucchini

This is one of my favorite summer sides from my days growing up in the South. If you are having trouble getting your kids to eat their green veggies, I can think of no sweeter introduction!

High-heat cooking oil for frying
1–2 large eggs, beaten (or ½ cup milk of choice)
1 cup cornmeal
⅓ cup granulated cane sugar
1 large zucchini, washed and sliced in thin circles

▸ Preheat an electric skillet to 375–400°F—or a griddle or frying pan to medium-high heat—and pour into it enough oil of your choice to cover the bottom of the pan to ⅛–¼-inch deep.

▸ Prepare two small bowls, one containing the egg and the other containing the cornmeal and sugar mixed together. Dip each zucchini slice in the egg, then dredge in the cornmeal mixture. Lay in the hot oil and fry just until each side is lightly browned and crispy, flipping to fry both sides. Keep the oil hot so that the zucchini cooks for only 1–2 minutes per side, or the zucchini will be mushy rather than crunchy.

▸ Lay the cooked zucchini circles onto a paper plate or platter covered with high-quality paper towels to cool slightly and absorb any extra oil. Serve warm.

SERVES 4

- -
Note: Depending on the size of your zucchini, you may need to double the dry ingredients and egg or milk to have enough to finish.
- -

Croutons

If you're truly getting into gluten-free baking, you'll undoubtedly be making and experimenting with several bread recipes. Some will work better than others, some will be devoured on the day they come out of the oven. For those that linger, freeze 'em! Then when you need some croutons for a recipe, or for that beautiful salad you're planning, you'll be halfway to crouton heaven.

> 3 thick slices of gluten-free bread (cut ¾-inch thick)
> 2 tablespoons extra-virgin olive oil
> 1 teaspoon dried oregano
> 1 teaspoon dried basil

▸ Preheat the oven to 375°F.

▸ Slice the bread into ¾-inch cubes and lay them out onto a foil-lined baking sheet. Bake for 15 minutes or until crispy on the edges (toss midway through to toast on all sides).

▸ Meanwhile, heat oil in a large saucepan to medium-high heat. Transfer the dried cubes to the hot oil and toss, sautéing until the oil is absorbed and the croutons are crunchy. Toss in the herbs and transfer to a bowl for serving with Gazpacho (see page 133) or in your favorite salad.

MAKES APPROXIMATELY 2 CUPS

See photo insert.

continues

Breadcrumbs

Breadcrumbs can be made from these croutons by simply pulsing them in a food processor or blender to the size you need for your recipe. Freeze any unused portions to be sure to have some on hand for future recipes. To add more seasonings, try this spicy recipe:

COATING:

½ cup dry bread cubes, gluten-free
¼ teaspoon red pepper (optional)
¼ teaspoon black pepper
¼ teaspoon garlic powder
¼ teaspoon sea salt
½ teaspoon dried parsley
⅛ teaspoon chili powder (optional)

▸ Stir ingredients together to mix well then pulse in a food processor or blender to the consistency you desire.

Fauxtatoes

(a.k.a. Mashed Cauliflower)

Healthier (more vitamins, minerals, and fiber) than traditional mashed potatoes, but no less tasty!

> 1 head of cauliflower
> 3–4 tablespoons butter or nondairy alternative
> Approximately ½ cup half-and-half or liquid nondairy creamer
> ½–¾ cup Parmesan-style cheese (dairy or nondairy)
> Salt and pepper, to taste

▶ Cut up the cauliflower into small pieces and steam just until tender. Drain the cauliflower and leave in a colander to cool.

▶ Put the cooled cauliflower into a food processor with the steel blade and pulse process several times. Add butter, ¼ cup of the half-and-half, and all of the cheese, processing until smooth. If too dry, add the remaining half-and-half until the cauliflower is the consistency of mashed potatoes. Add salt and pepper to taste.

Variation: For added flavor, toss in steamed or sautéed mushrooms, onions, and/or bell peppers when or after you put the cauliflower in the food processor, depending on how well you would like to hide these veggies!

SERVES 6

Fried Green Tomatoes

These salty and tart treats are a meal for me on many a summer night, and they are wonderful as sandwiches for lunch as well (see Hamburger and Hot Dog Buns recipe, page 113). I learned about these early in my childhood in the South and have tried to indoctrinate northern friends along the way, most of whom, I'm happy to say, have been pleasantly surprised at how delicious these unassuming and tender discs can be! Another in the category of "You can't judge a book by its cover!"

The key to this summertime delicacy is in selecting the tomatoes. If you grow your own, that's fantastic! Otherwise, hit the local farmers' market or pick-your-own farm and opt for large, very firm, green tomatoes. If you do not use them right away, store in the produce drawer of your refrigerator to slow the ripening. Once they get softer and turn a pale whitish-green, then red color, they are too ripe for this recipe—they will fall apart and never get crisp because they are too juicy.

Once you select the right tomatoes, be sure your oil is hot enough. If it is not hot enough to get the batter on the tomatoes crispy, it will just make the tomatoes mushy—likewise, it's best not to make them too far in advance of serving because they are prone to lose their crispness when sitting out for too long. However, you can refrigerate or freeze fried tomatoes by cooling them, then layering them between wax paper and sealing them in a zip-top bag. The best way to serve again after refrigeration or freezing is to quick-broil them to restore their crispiness.

High heat cooking oil
1 cup Jules Gluten Free All Purpose Flour (pages 6, 8)
1¼ teaspoons salt
¼ teaspoon cracked black pepper
2–3 medium-large firm green tomatoes

continues

- Heat enough oil in a large skillet to cover the entire skillet bottom. While that is coming to high heat (400°F), prepare a bowl for dredging with the flour, salt, and pepper whisked together well. If necessary, double the dry ingredients for dredging the tomatoes to be sure to have enough to coat all the slices.

- Slice the tomatoes approximately ¼-inch thick, removing as much peel as possible from the two end pieces, as the flour mixture will not stick well to the skins. Dredge each slice through the flour mixture, coating each side well, then lay gently in the heated oil. Cook on both sides until light brown and crispy (approximately 2 minutes per side if the oil is at the proper temperature).

- Remove to a paper towel– or parchment-lined baking sheet and put into a 200°F oven to keep warm until serving.

SERVES 4

"Fried" Onions

For a traditional Green Bean Casserole (page 84), fry up your own onions with Jules Gluten Free All Purpose Flour and your favorite recipe. For a slightly healthier version, try these baked ("fried") onions.

> 1 medium onion, sliced thinly
> ⅓ cup Jules Gluten Free All Purpose Flour (pages 6, 8)
> ¼ teaspoon sea salt

▸ Preheat the oven to 475°F. Spray a baking sheet with cooking spray and set aside.

▸ Combine the sliced onions and dry ingredients in a large bowl, tossing until totally coated with flour. Pour out onto baking sheet and separate the onion ring slices so they are not touching each other too much. Bake for 15–20 minutes, tossing one or two times while cooking to golden brown.

▸ Remove them when cooked and set them aside while you are making the green bean casserole or other dish. Double this recipe if making for a munching snack.

MAKES ENOUGH FOR ONE CASSEROLE

Gravy

Gravy can be as simple as pan drippings or caramelized onions, Jules Gluten Free All Purpose Flour, broth, and seasonings. This recipe is loosely written, as gravy flavors can be very different depending on your tastes. As long as you get the roux right, the seasonings are easy to add or alter, depending on your own taste.

> 2 tablespoons roasted turkey drippings (omit if making vegetarian)
> 1 large onion plus 2 tablespoons butter or nondairy alternative for sautéing (if making vegetarian)
> 2 tablespoons butter or nondairy alternative
> 2 tablespoons Jules Gluten Free All Purpose Flour (pages 6, 8)
> 2 cups chicken or vegetable stock, gluten-free
> Salt and pepper, to taste
> Dry white wine (optional)

▸ If using turkey drippings, after the turkey has been roasted, pour the juices from the turkey into a large measuring cup. Skim off the fat and set the juices aside.

▸ If making without turkey drippings (vegetarian method), dice a large onion and slowly cook it in a saucepan with 2 tablespoons of butter over low heat until the onions have caramelized and are lightly browned.

▸ Using either method, in a separate saucepan, make a roux using equal parts butter and gluten-free flour.

▸ Begin by slowly heating the butter over low-medium heat until it melts, whisk in the flour, breaking up any lumps, and continue stirring in circles with a wooden spoon until it thickens and is a light yellow-brown color. Do not let it burn!

▸ At this point, slowly stir in the stock, approximately 1½–2 cups; stir to combine and thicken slightly, raising the heat to medium and stirring until thickened and bubbly.

▸ Finally, add the cooked onions or turkey drippings, and season further to taste with salt and pepper. Add dry white wine to thin the gravy, if necessary.

SERVES 2

Green Bean Casserole

With a few substitutions, you can still enjoy your favorite Thanksgiving Day side dishes, like green bean casserole. Progresso Cream of Mushroom Soup and Health Valley Organic Cream of Mushroom Soup are two currently gluten-free options. For a gluten- and dairy-free option, Imagine Foods Mushroom Soup is a wonderful ingredient option.

> 1 recipe "Fried" Onions (page 82), or Funyuns, which are currently gluten-free
>
> 1 pound green beans—canned, frozen, or fresh (rinsed, trimmed, and halved)
>
> 2 tablespoons unsalted butter or nondairy alternative
>
> 2 large portobello mushrooms, diced
>
> ½ teaspoon freshly ground black pepper
>
> ½ teaspoon garlic powder
>
> ¼ teaspoon ground nutmeg
>
> 2 tablespoons Jules Gluten Free All Purpose Flour (pages 6, 8)
>
> ⅓ cup sour cream (dairy or nondairy) or plain coconut yogurt
>
> 2 cups cream of mushroom soup (dairy or nondairy)

▸ Heat the oven to 400°F. If using fresh beans, boil in lightly salted water for 5 minutes, then rinse with cold water and drain. If using canned or frozen beans, rinse and set aside.

▸ In a large saucepan, melt the butter and toss in the diced mushrooms and pepper. Stir over medium heat for 5 minutes, then add the spices and flour, stirring to coat. Cook an additional minute then add the sour cream and soup and lower the heat to medium-low. Cook while the mixture thickens, at least 5–8 minutes more.

▸ Remove from the heat and stir in half of the fried onions and all of the drained beans. Pour the mixture into a large casserole and cook for 10 minutes or until bubbly. Sprinkle the remaining onions on top and bake for an additional 5 minutes. Serve warm.

SERVES 8

Guacamole

This recipe makes enough for a large party, but it's so delicious that it goes fast! It is simple to halve the recipe, though, if your group is somewhat small. Guacamole doesn't keep well for long in the refrigerator, as it can turn an un-appetizing brown hue in a short time, so make it shortly before you intend to serve it. To help preserve any leftovers, stir ½ teaspoon of lemon juice into the dip and cover tightly before refrigerating.

> 6 ripe Haas avocados (avocados are ripe when the skins are black, but make sure they are not yet mushy)
> 1 sweet Vidalia onion, diced
> 1 tablespoon garlic, diced
> 3 small fresh Roma tomatoes or 2 medium vine ripe tomatoes, diced (you may also use ripe yellow or orange tomatoes)
> Black pepper, to taste
> ½ teaspoon cumin
> ¾ teaspoon (or more) coarse sea salt
> 1 bunch fresh cilantro, slightly chopped (optional)
> Juice from ½ a lime (no seeds)

▸ Peel and chop the avocado or mash if you prefer a smoother texture. Add the onions, garlic, and tomatoes. Mix well. Add pepper, cumin, and salt and mix again. Taste to see if more salt is needed and add it in ¼ teaspoon increments until the taste is right. Snip fresh cilantro leaves and discard the stalks. Stir in the leaves and lime juice.

▸ Chill for 30 minutes then serve with chips, chili, or other Mexican dishes.

SERVES 10

Hushpuppies or Crab Fritters

This recipe is a wonderful base for traditional hushpuppies, or mix it up a bit and introduce something new like fresh okra, crabmeat, and gluten-free beer—I like Green's Quest Tripel Blonde Ale in this recipe. If you want to try this recipe without these added elements, just make the base recipe and leave out the Cajun seasonings, crab, and okra to have a light, fluffy, crunchy, savory, and delicious hushpuppy!

2 cups yellow or white cornmeal, gluten-free
1 cup Jules Gluten Free All Purpose Flour (pages 6, 8)
4 teaspoons baking powder, gluten-free
1 teaspoon salt
4 teaspoons granulated cane sugar
1 teaspoon Creole seasoning (e.g., Konriko Creole Seasoning)—if making crab fritters
¾–1 cup okra, chopped (if making crab fritters)
1 cup lump crabmeat (if making crab fritters)
2 large eggs or egg substitute of choice (like Ener-G Egg Replacer or Egg Substitute #1, 2, or 7, pages 15–16), beaten
1½ cups gluten-free beer (or club soda)
High heat cooking oil for frying

▸ Sift the dry ingredients together in a large bowl. Add in the okra and crabmeat if making crab fritters.

▸ Add the eggs and beer, mixing until moistened. Let stand while the oil heats.

▸ Add oil to a large pot or Dutch oven to a depth of at least 3–4 inches. Heat the oil to 350°F or medium high flame.

▸ Drop the batter by large tablespoonfuls into heated oil; fry 2–3 minutes per side or until golden brown and floating. Remove with a slotted spoon and drain on paper plates or a wire rack until cool enough to eat.

▸ Serve immediately.

MAKES APPROXIMATELY 4 DOZEN FRITTERS, DEPENDING ON THE SIZE

Mango Avocado Salsa

The world over, mangoes and avocado seem to end up together. The combination is beautiful as a dip, over fish, or in a salad, and healthy to boot. Use more or less Tabasco according to your penchant for heat.

1 large mango, peeled and diced
1 large ripe Haas avocado, peeled and diced
1 cup black beans, rinsed
½ ear cooked corn, cut off the cob
2 tablespoons fresh lime juice
1 small bunch fresh cilantro, chopped
Approximately ¾ teaspoon Tabasco
½ teaspoon cumin
¼ teaspoon coarse sea salt

▸ Combine all ingredients in a large bowl and gently toss together to combine. Taste to determine if you like more spice.

▸ Serve with corn tortilla chips, Golden Potato Latkes (page 158), Fish Tacos (page 149), or over grilled white fish like tilapia, orange roughy, or flounder.

SERVES 4

Mashed Potatoes

Sometimes it is helpful to recall that old homemade favorites are and always have been gluten-free. Keep this recipe in your rotation, adding other veggies and savory elements once in awhile just to keep things interesting!

3–4 pounds Idaho potatoes
1 parsnip, 3–4 chopped mushrooms, 1 cup chopped broccoli florets,
    or other vegetables (optional, but healthy!)
Salt and pepper, to taste
¼–½ teaspoon garlic salt
½ cup sour cream (dairy or nondairy) or plain coconut yogurt
2 tablespoons butter or nondairy alternative
Milk (dairy or nondairy)
Parsley

▸ Peel and cube potatoes and parsnip (if using). If you like the skins on your potatoes, do not peel.

▸ Boil the potatoes and parsnips (if using) until fork tender; do not let the potatoes get mushy. Drain the water off and mash with a potato masher or a stand mixer. Add salt (begin with ½ teaspoon), pepper (begin with ¼ teaspoon), and garlic salt (begin with ¼ teaspoon). Taste before adding too much—you can always add more, but you can't take it away! Sauté any other optional vegetables separately and set aside.

▸ Next, blend the sour cream, then the butter with the potatoes. Begin adding milk until the mash reaches your preferred consistency. Add parsley and any additional salt, pepper, and garlic salt desired. Stir in other cooked vegetables. You may have to add more milk if the potatoes stand for long before serving.

SERVES 6–8

Matzo

This recipe makes a great saltine-like cracker that is wonderful for Jewish holidays or any time of year, for that matter!

> 1 cup Jules Gluten Free All Purpose Flour (pages 6, 8)
> ½ cup almond flour or buckwheat flour
> ½ teaspoon coarse-ground sea salt or kosher salt
> 4 tablespoons extra-virgin olive oil
> 3 tablespoons water
> Coarse-ground sea salt or kosher salt for tops

▶ Preheat the oven to 450°F (static) or 425°F (convection, preferred).

▶ Whisk together the flours and salt, then add in the liquid slowly while stirring with a fork or pastry cutter. If the dough is too dry, add additional water by the ½ teaspoonful to get dough wet enough that it will form a ball but not be sticky.

▶ Form a ball with the dough and pat out onto a piece of parchment paper cut to the size of your baking sheet and dusted with gluten-free flour. Press with your fingers to flatten the dough to the thickness of matzo, then prick all over with a fork. Sprinkle with additional salt, if desired.

▶ Bake for 10 minutes, or just until slightly browned.

SERVES 4

Salty and Sweet Party Mix

For a personalized version of this great, versatile mix, you can use the nuts of your choice (or no nuts at all, or seeds, for that matter). As always, though, because manufacturing practices change, read the labels of the pretzels and cereals you're considering, to make sure they're (still) certified gluten-free.

> 2 cups halved pecans (omit if making nut-free, or use mixed seeds like pepitas/pumpkin and sunflower)
> ¼ cup butter or nondairy alternative
> ⅛ cup granulated cane sugar
> 1½ cups gluten-free pretzel sticks (e.g., Glutino Brand)
> 1½ cups gluten-free pretzel twists (e.g., Glutino Brand)
> 2 cups gluten-free cereal (e.g., Chex cereal—Rice, Corn, Honey Nut, Chocolate, or Cinnamon varieties)
> 1 cup salted cashews or mixed nuts (omit if avoiding nuts)
> 1 cup chocolate chips, gluten-free (dairy or nondairy, e.g., Enjoy Life or Sunspire)

▶ Lightly brown pecans or seeds in a skillet with melted butter over low heat. Add sugar, stirring until the sugar dissolves and the pecans are slightly shiny.

▶ Pour pecans or seeds onto a cookie sheet lined with paper towels. Spread over the paper towels, pat, then pour onto another unlined cookie sheet to cool (do not let cool on the paper towels or they will stick to the towels). Toss cooled nuts/seeds together with the other ingredients in a large bowl. Mix and serve.

YIELDS 9 CUPS OF MIX

Quinoa Salad—Italian Style

This ancient grain should have a permanent space on one of your kitchen shelves. It's a nearly complete food, nutritionally, and can largely be used in place of rice, if you're looking to up your protein and other vitamins and minerals. And it's so refreshing right out of the fridge . . . perfect for a picnic or as a side to a sandwich for lunch on a hot summer's day.

1½ cups dry quinoa (rinsed)
1 teaspoon fresh garlic, minced
½ cup plus 3 tablespoons extra-virgin olive oil
1 cup chopped onion
½ cup chopped red, orange, or yellow bell pepper
1 cup chopped tomato
¼ cup balsamic vinegar
2 tablespoons fresh lemon juice plus lemon zest
2 cups Italian parsley, leaves only, chopped
2 teaspoons sea salt
¼ teaspoon ground pepper

▸ Prepare rinsed quinoa according to package directions.

▸ In a large pan, sauté the garlic and onions in 3 tablespoons of olive oil for 3–4 minutes, then add the peppers. Add the tomatoes last and cook until the peppers are lightly browned. Combine the cooked quinoa and vegetables in a large bowl and stir together with the ½ cup of olive oil, balsamic vinegar, lemon juice, zest, parsley, salt, and pepper.

▸ Toss well, refrigerate, and serve chilled or make Stuffed Peppers with Quinoa (see page 163).

SERVES 4

Quinoa Salad—Mexican Style

You can vary this versatile recipe by what you have or don't have on hand. Make it to appeal to the most people in your house, and you'll feel great knowing the nutrition they're getting with every helping.

1 cup dry quinoa (rinsed)
1 clove garlic, minced
½–¾ cup chopped yellow onion
⅓ cup plus 2 tablespoons extra-virgin olive oil
1 large red, orange, or yellow bell pepper, chopped
1 (16-ounce) can kidney beans, rinsed
1 (15-ounce) can black beans, rinsed
1½ cups cooked corn kernels
1 cup chopped tomato
½–1 teaspoon chili powder
1 teaspoon cumin
½ teaspoon ground pepper
¾ teaspoon sea salt
⅓ cup red wine vinegar
⅓ cup minced fresh cilantro

▸ Prepare rinsed quinoa according to package directions.

▸ In a large pan, sauté the garlic and onion in 2 tablespoons of olive oil for 3–4 minutes, or until the onions are translucent, then add the peppers, cooking just until the peppers are lightly browned. Add to the cooked quinoa, beans, corn, tomatoes, and spices, together with the ⅓ cup of olive oil, red wine vinegar, and cilantro.

▸ Toss well, refrigerate, and serve chilled, with chips, on salad, or make Stuffed Peppers with Quinoa (see page 163).

SERVES 4

Chunky Shrimp or Fish Dip

Hot sauce, cilantro, and avocado were just begging for a little shrimp to round them out for the perfect dip. Throw this together in minutes the next time you entertain and your guests will talk about it for hours.

1 pound medium cooked, deveined shrimp, cut into thirds (or firm white fish like red snapper, orange roughy, cod, grouper, halibut, or mahi mahi, cooked and cut into bite-size chunks)

6 ounces ketchup, chili sauce, or cocktail sauce

1–2 small ripe Haas avocados, peeled and cubed

2 tablespoons chopped fresh cilantro leaves

1 large tomato, diced

2–3 ounces black olives, chopped (optional)

½ medium red or purple onion, diced

Dash of Tabasco sauce

▸ Stir all ingredients together gently in a medium-size bowl.

▸ Cover and chill until ready to serve.

▸ Serve cold with corn tortilla chips.

SERVES 4

Traditional Stuffing

Don't let a special occasion go by without stuffing simply because you're eating gluten-free. Show up with this dish at your family function and no one will notice it's free from anything . . . unless you tell them.

6 cups white bread cubes, gluten-free
    (approximately ½ of a 3-pound loaf;
    see page 102)
3 tablespoons extra-virgin olive oil
½ cup diced onion
½ teaspoon ground nutmeg
2 teaspoons sage
½ teaspoon marjoram
½ teaspoon salt
1 teaspoon pepper

1 cup chopped carrots
1 cup chopped celery
2 cups peeled and chopped apples
    (optional)
¼ cup dried cranberries (optional)
½ cup pecans or walnuts, chopped
    (optional; omit if making nut-free)
¼ cup flaxseed meal
Approximately 2 cups chicken or vegetable
    stock, gluten-free

▸ Preheat the oven to 300°F.

▸ Cut bread slices into ¾-inch cubes and spread in a single layer onto a cookie sheet lined with aluminum foil. Bake for 20–25 minutes, tossing during cook time, or until the cubes are dried out.

▸ In a large skillet, heat the oil over medium-high heat, then add the onion, stirring until tender and translucent and browning a bit at the edges. Next add the spices, carrots, and celery, sautéing an additional 2–3 minutes. Set aside.

▸ Preheat the oven to 375°F (static).

▸ Pour the dried bread cubes into a 9 x 13-inch baking pan. Stir in the sautéed vegetables and distribute throughout the cubes. Add the apples, cranberries, nuts (if using), and flaxseed meal last, stirring well, but gently. Drizzle the stock over the mixture, stirring to coat all the cubes. You may find you need slightly more or less broth to accomplish this.

▸ Cover with foil and bake at 375°F for approximately 30 minutes. If you want your stuffing crispy on top, bake without the foil, or remove the foil for the last 10 minutes of baking.

SERVES 8–10

See photo insert.

Candied Sweet Potato Mash

A delicious side dish option that is simple, nutritious, and delicious.

2 pounds sweet potatoes (approximately 3 medium)

½ cup brown sugar

3 tablespoons butter or nondairy alternative

3 tablespoons water

½ teaspoon salt

¼ cup walnuts or pecans, toasted (optional; omit if making nut-free)

¼ cup dried cranberries, raisins, or cherries

1–2 apples with skin on, chopped (firm baking apples like Gala, Fuji, Winesap Golden Delicious, or Honey Crisp, not tart apples)

▸ Peel and cube the sweet potatoes and add to a pot with enough boiling salted water to cover the potatoes.

▸ Cover the pot, letting potatoes boil until tender, 30–35 minutes. (Another option is to wash and pierce the whole potatoes with a fork and bake in microwave until fork tender. Let cool, then slip off the skins. When cooled, cut into small chunks.)

▸ Mix brown sugar, butter, water, and salt in an 8-inch skillet. Cook over medium heat while stirring, until bubbly. Add the sweet potato chunks and stir until glazed. Stir in the nuts, berries, and apples until well mixed.

SERVES 6

Sweet Potato Soufflé

Sweet potatoes are one of the most versatile, healthy, and yummy staples in a gluten-free diet. In recipes like this, they add flavor to this super-easy casserole that can be enjoyed hot out of the oven or cold straight from the pan as leftovers! For an extra time-saver, use canned sweet potatoes in lieu of boiling and peeling, if time doesn't permit.

3 cups cooked, peeled, and mashed sweet potatoes
(or canned and drained)
1 teaspoon gluten-free vanilla extract
2 eggs, slightly beaten, or egg substitute of choice
(like Ener-G Egg Replacer or Egg Substitute #1, 2, 3, or 4, page 15)
1 cup granulated cane sugar
2 tablespoons melted butter or nondairy alternative
½ cup milk (dairy or nondairy)
2 teaspoons cinnamon
½ teaspoon nutmeg

TOPPING:

1 cup light or dark brown sugar
½ cup chopped pecans (omit if avoiding nuts)
⅓ cup Jules Gluten Free All Purpose Flour (pages 6, 8)
¼ cup melted butter or nondairy alternative
½ cup coconut, flaked (optional)

▸ Preheat the oven to 325°F.

▸ Put all the casserole ingredients into a large mixing bowl and beat on medium speed until smooth. Pour into an oiled 9 x 13-inch casserole dish and set aside. Prepare the topping by combining all the ingredients and mixing by hand. Sprinkle over the top of the casserole and bake for 50 minutes.

SERVES 8

Roasted Vegetable Sticks

I never cease to be amazed at the finicky little kids, the picky teenagers, and other veggie avoiders who stand around and eat these right off the cookie sheet. Make plenty, if you expect to have any left for yourself.

> 1 pound broccoli and/or cauliflower florets, separated into bite-size stalks, or "sticks"
> 1-inch piece fresh ginger root, peeled and diced
> ½ teaspoon sea salt
> 1 teaspoon red pepper flakes (optional)
> 2 tablespoons extra-virgin olive oil
> Black pepper, to taste

▸ Preheat the oven to medium broil.

▸ Wash the broccoli and cauliflower florets. Toss them in a large zip-top bag with the remaining ingredients to coat. Prepare a baking sheet by lining with aluminum foil and spraying with olive or canola oil spray.

▸ Spread the florets onto the sheet and broil for only 4 or 5 minutes, until lightly crispy, stirring often so they won't burn.

▸ Serve warm.

SERVES 6

3

Breads
and Rolls*

---

* Note: These recipes may be mixed by hand with a fork and very strong muscles, but it is ideal to use a stand mixer with a mixing paddle, not a dough hook. Some recipes are also written with bread machine directions as an option. See Baking Notes, page 27, for more information on baking gluten-free breads.

Crusty French Baguette

While it is possible to roll this wet dough into a traditional baguette shape by hand, it is far easier to "cheat" and simply scoop the dough into a gallon-size zip-top bag, snip one bottom corner out, pipe the dough into a baguette pan, then just toss the bag for easy cleanup. Voilà!

1 teaspoon granulated cane sugar

2¼ teaspoons (1 packet) rapid rise yeast, gluten-free

1¼ cups very warm water

2¼ cups Jules Gluten Free All Purpose Flour (pages 6, 8)

1 teaspoon sea salt

Cornmeal

Milk (dairy or nondairy) or mixed egg wash for brushing on uncooked loaf
(the milk will help to brown the loaf; an egg stirred with a tablespoon
of water will make the loaf shiny and lightly browned)

▸ Prepare a proofing area to let your loaf rise; a good option is to place the loaf in a pre-heated 200°F oven after it has been turned off. If you have a baguette pan, line it with foil then spray with nonstick cooking spray and sprinkle with cornmeal. If you are using a cookie sheet instead, line it with foil and sprinkle cornmeal onto the foil, then line up two dowels or other forms to help keep the bread in the long thin shape while it's rising and cooking; wrap these dowels with aluminum foil and spray all the foil with cooking oil.

▸ In a small bowl, mix the sugar, yeast, and very warm water and set aside to proof for 5 minutes (if, after 5 minutes, the yeast is not bubbling, throw it out and start again with fresh yeast).

▸ In a large mixing bowl, whisk together the gluten-free flour and salt. With the beater blade or dough hook on your mixer, slowly work in the yeast mixture with the flour and salt.

▸ Once fully integrated, beat an additional 2 minutes on medium-high. The dough will be very wet at this point.

▸ Scoop the dough into a gallon-size zip-top bag with 2 inches cut from a bottom corner of the bag.

▸ Squeeze the bag to remove the air then squeeze the dough through the cut hole to form one long loaf in your prepared baguette pan or in between your prepared dowels on the parchment-lined cookie sheet.

continues

- Gently brush the milk or mixed egg wash all over the exposed areas of the loaf with a pastry brush.

- Cover the loaf with wax paper sprayed with cooking spray and set it in your warmed oven or other proofing spot for 20 minutes.

- Preheat the oven to 400°F and place a baking pan with water onto the bottom shelf of the oven. Leave this pan in the oven during the baking process as well—the humidity created by this heated water will help the bread to form an extra crunchy crust.

- Once risen, uncover the baguette and make 3 or 4 diagonal cuts into the dough with a serrated knife, cutting approximately ¼ inch deep. Using a clean spray bottle, spritz the dough well with water before baking.

- Bake for 20 minutes and brush the top of the bread with milk or egg wash again, then bake for 20 minutes more, or until a toothpick inserted into the bread comes out clean and the internal temperature of the bread is 205–210°F.

- Remove from pan and cool on a wire rack until ready to serve.

MAKES 1 LOAF

(OR SEVERAL SMALLER LOAVES IF DOUGH IS PIPED INTO SHORTER FORMS)

See photo insert.

Beer Bread or Dinner Rolls

I used Green's Quest Tripel Blonde Gluten Free Ale in this recipe to add flavor, but many carbonated beverages would serve the same purpose—carbonation assists in rise with yeast breads. I also used some buckwheat flour to enhance the flavor and nutritional value, but you could simply use my Jules Gluten Free All Purpose Flour for all of the flour required if you don't have any buckwheat flour handy, or if your kids demand a truly white bread!

> 3 large eggs, room temperature, or egg substitute of choice, such as two recipes Egg Substitute #1 (page 15) plus one recipe Egg Substitute #7 (page 16)
> 3 tablespoons extra-virgin olive oil
> 2 tablespoons honey or agave nectar (omit if using ginger ale)
> 2¾ cups Jules Gluten Free All Purpose Flour (pages 6, 8)
> ¼ cup buckwheat flour (or you may use an equal amount of Jules Gluten Free All Purpose Flour)
> 1 teaspoon salt
> 1 tablespoon granulated cane sugar
> 10 ounces gluten-free ale, club soda, ginger ale, or Perrier
> 2¼ teaspoons (1 packet) rapid rise or bread machine yeast, gluten-free
> Toppings such as coarse sea salt, sesame seeds, grated cheese, etc. (optional)

▸ Prepare 1 loaf pan or 12 popover pans by oiling lightly.

▸ In a large mixing bowl, whisk together the eggs, oil, and honey.

▸ In another large bowl, whisk flours, salt, and sugar. With the mixer on low speed, slowly pour the dry ingredients into the liquids to combine. Continue beating while slowly pouring in the ale to mix. Once incorporated, add the yeast. Beat until the batter is smooth, then increase mixing speed and beat for 4 minutes. (Note: I say "batter," not "dough," because this recipe does not make a stiff bread dough.)

▸ Pour the batter into the loaf pan or, using a large ice cream scoop, measure batter and scoop equal portions into the prepared popover pans. Sprinkle with any toppings at this point.

continues

- Cover with a damp towel or oiled wax paper and let rise in a warm, moist place for 30 minutes (an oven preheated to 200°F, then turned off, with a bowl of water in the oven to add moisture, is a good option).

- Once the bread has risen, bake at 375°F (static) or 350°F (convection) for approximately 35 minutes for the loaf or 15 minutes for the rolls. The internal temperature of the loaf should be 205–210°F. The bread or rolls should have risen high above the tops of the pans and be golden brown with a nice crust. Remove from the oven and cool in the pans for 5 minutes, then gently remove from the pans and serve warm. Be sure to let the bread cool well before wrapping tightly or keeping in an airtight container for storage.

MAKES 1 LOAF OR 12 DINNER ROLLS

Buttermilk Biscuits

I never make enough of these, either at home or when I'm using them as samples. That's because you can't tell the difference between these and the ones you fondly recall from your past—even in their dairy-free form. Try them. You won't be disappointed.

2 cups Jules Gluten Free All Purpose Flour (pages 6, 8)
2 teaspoons baking powder, gluten-free
½ teaspoon baking soda
1 teaspoon coarse sea salt
¼ cup powdered buttermilk (or powdered dairy or nondairy milk and
    add ½ teaspoon apple cider vinegar to the half-and-half)
4 tablespoons butter or nondairy alternative
½ cup half-and-half (or unflavored liquid nondairy creamer)
½ cup sour cream (dairy or nondairy) or coconut yogurt
Butter or nondairy alternative to spread on the biscuit tops before baking

▸ Preheat the oven to 375°F (static) or 350°F (convection, preferred).

▸ Whisk together the dry ingredients in a large bowl. Cut the butter into the dry ingredients with a pastry cutter or in a food processor until you achieve the consistency of coarse meal. Add the half-and-half and sour cream and stir with a fork to thoroughly combine.

▸ Pat the dough onto a lightly floured (with gluten-free flour) counter or pastry mat, forming a 6- to 7-inch disc shape, approximately 1 inch thick. Dip a biscuit cutter into your flour and cut out approximately 9 biscuits (cut straight down, do not twist the cutter).

▸ Transfer to a parchment-lined baking sheet and prick the tops with a fork a few times. Lay a small, thin pat of butter or nondairy alternative on the top of each biscuit before baking.

▸ Bake for approximately 14 minutes or until the tops are lightly browned and they are firm, but not hard. It is important not to overbake them!

MAKES 9 BISCUITS, DEPENDING ON SIZE

Challah

This braided bread looks fancy and very difficult to make, but it's deceptively easy! Because there is no gluten in the dough, it can be mixed and braided immediately, left to rise once, then baked. The flour mixture gives the dough enough elasticity to be easily braided into two long loaves or crowns. If you would rather, simply fill muffin cups or popover trays with dough and bake as dinner rolls instead. Versatile, easy, and delicious—the best kind of recipe!

> ⅓ cup warm water
> 2¼ teaspoons (1 packet) rapid rise yeast, gluten-free
> 1 teaspoon granulated cane sugar
> 1 cup vanilla yogurt (dairy or nondairy), at room temperature
> 1 teaspoon apple cider vinegar
> 5 large egg yolks at room temperature (slightly mixed)
> ⅓ cup canola oil
> 4 tablespoons honey, agave nectar, or molasses
> 4 cups Jules Gluten Free All Purpose Flour (pages 6, 8)
> 3 tablespoons plus 2 teaspoons granulated cane sugar
> 1¼ teaspoons kosher salt
> ½ teaspoon baking soda
> 2 teaspoons gluten-free baking powder
> 1 large egg, mixed with 1 tablespoon water (to brush on top of loaves)
> Poppy seeds, sesame seeds, raisins, coarse sea salt, or other gluten-free
>   topping (optional)

▶ Preheat the oven to 200°F, then turn it off; if you have a warming drawer, set it to low/moist setting instead. Prepare a baking sheet by lining it with parchment paper.

▶ In a small bowl, mix together the warm water, yeast, and 1 teaspoon of sugar to proof the yeast; set aside. In the bowl of your stand mixer, add the other wet ingredients and mix until combined. Whisk together the dry ingredients in a separate bowl.

▶ After 5 minutes of proofing, stir in the yeast mixture into the wet ingredients (note: if yeast isn't bubbling at this point, throw it out and start again with fresh yeast). Gradually stir in the dry ingredients until fully integrated, then mix 2 minutes more on medium speed.

continues

- Once the dough is well mixed, divide it in half and divide each half again into three equal-size balls (total 6 balls of dough). Roll each ball out into a coil or long log on a clean, flat surface dusted lightly with gluten-free flour or cornstarch.

- Pinch together one end of each of the three coils, wetting the ends slightly with water to help them join together at the top, then braid them, finishing by connecting them together as you did the top of the braid, or connecting to the top of the other end to form a crown.

- Gently transfer the loaf or crown to a parchment-lined baking sheet. Repeat for the second set of three balls.

- In the alternative, simply divide the dough in half, roll out into a flattened coil, then twist upon itself and join at the ends to form a circular loaf; repeat with the other half of the dough ball.

- In a small bowl, mix the extra egg together with water and brush it over each loaf well, coating the entire exposed surface. Sprinkle the seeds or any toppings on the loaves at this point, then cover the loaves with wax paper sprayed with cooking oil or damp towels. Place the sheet in a warming drawer set to low heat, or into the preheated oven for 20–30 minutes. (Don't expect the bread to rise much at this stage).

- Once risen slightly, place the uncovered tray in an oven preheated to 350°F (static) or 325°F (convection) for 20–25 minutes. Remove to cool on a wire rack and cut after slightly cooled.

MAKES 2 LOAVES OR CROWNS

See photo insert.

Cornbread

I've combined both sweet and savory styles of cornbread in this recipe. The result is a savory, light, and fluffy corn cake with a kick that enhances wonderful foods like my Butternut Squash Soup (see page 130). I also added a chipotle chile pepper, but you could use a different kind of chile or pepper, or feel free to ignore my mix-ins altogether—this won't upset the finished product, it will only change the taste and texture.

3 tablespoons butter or nondairy alternative

1 cup sour cream (dairy or nondairy) or coconut yogurt

¾ cup milk (dairy or nondairy)

1 large egg (or egg substitute like Ener-G Egg Replacer, reconstituted, or Egg Substitute #7, page 16)

1 cup yellow cornmeal, gluten-free

2 tablespoons flaxseed meal (optional)

1 cup Jules Gluten Free All Purpose Flour (pages 6, 8)

1 tablespoon baking powder, gluten-free

½ teaspoon baking soda

½ teaspoon salt

4 tablespoons granulated cane sugar (add more or less, to taste)

1–2 chipotle peppers or ⅛ cup diced jalapeños (optional)

¼–½ cup cooked corn kernels (optional)

▸ Preheat the oven to 400°F (static).

▸ Place the butter in a heavy 10-inch cast iron skillet or 9-inch square baking pan; place in the oven to melt and warm the skillet while preparing the batter.

▸ Whisk together the sour cream, milk, and egg. In a separate bowl, combine the cornmeal, flaxseed meal, gluten-free flour, baking powder, baking soda, salt, and sugar.

▸ Stir the wet mixture into the dry ingredients. Fold in the chopped peppers and corn kernels, if using. Spread in the hot greased skillet or baking pan.

▸ Bake for 25–30 minutes, until set and crispy brown around the edges. Cool in the pan on a wire rack; cut into squares or wedges, depending on the shape of your pan.

SERVES 8

Crescent Rolls

As you can see from the short ingredient list, this recipe is divinely simple . . . like a crescent roll should be. They're great complements to many, many meals. Serve warm!

⅓ cup warm water
1 teaspoon granulated cane sugar
2¼ teaspoons (1 packet) rapid rise yeast
1⅓ cups plus 2 tablespoons Jules Gluten Free All Purpose Flour (pages 6, 8)
½ teaspoon salt
2 tablespoons honey or light agave nectar
1 egg or egg substitute of choice (like Egg Substitute #1 or 2, page 15)
Melted butter or nondairy alternative to brush onto rolls before baking

▶ In a large bowl, mix the warm water, sugar, and yeast and let stand for 5 minutes. If it does not bubble at this point, throw it out and repeat the proofing step with fresh yeast.

▶ Whisk together the flour and salt and set aside. Stir to combine the honey and egg in a separate bowl, then add the dry ingredients together with the yeast mixture and beat on the low speed of an electric mixer for 2–3 minutes, or until well-blended. The dough will be very wet.

▶ Turn the dough onto a well-floured pastry mat or clean counter and cut into 6 balls. Pat each ball into an elongated triangle shape, cutting the edges to form an even isosceles triangle and gathering the trimmings to make one more roll.

▶ Brush melted butter onto the dough at this point, then, from the wide end of the dough triangle, begin gently rolling the dough into a log, until the narrow tip of the triangle wraps around the roll on top.

▶ Place each roll onto a parchment-lined cookie sheet and pull the ends of each roll in toward the center to form a crescent shape.

▶ Cover with a damp towel or sheet of wax paper sprayed with cooking oil and place for 30 minutes in a warming drawer or oven preheated to 200°F, then turned off.

▶ Preheat the oven to 375°F (static) or 350°F (convection).

▶ Brush the tops of the risen rolls with melted butter. Bake for 10 minutes, or until light golden brown. Do not overbake.

continues

Pigs in a Blanket

To make this popular kid food, simply place a gluten-free hot dog (or vegetarian hot dog) at the wide end of the triangle of dough before rolling up, and roll to enclose the "pig" in the "blanket" of dough by rolling it up to the small end of the dough.

▸ Rise and bake as directed on page 108.

MAKES 6–8 ROLLS

Dinner Rolls/Breadsticks

If you recall the amazing smell of yeast rolls filling your house and yearn to relive that memory, yearn no longer! Make this versatile recipe your own by topping with different seasoned salts, cheese, chopped nuts, seeds, or other variations to accompany your meals.

2 cups Jules Gluten Free All Purpose Flour (pages 6, 8)

3 tablespoons flaxseed meal (optional, but recommended)

¼ cup milk powder (dairy or nondairy)

½ teaspoon baking soda

2 teaspoons baking powder, gluten-free

Pinch of salt

¼ cup shortening

1 teaspoon apple cider vinegar

3 tablespoons honey or agave nectar

2 large eggs or egg substitute of choice (like Egg Substitute #1, page 15)

2/3 cup vanilla yogurt (dairy or nondairy)

2¼ teaspoons (1 packet) rapid rise yeast

Milk (dairy or nondairy), egg white with 1 tablespoon water, *or* olive oil for brushing on tops

Gluten-free toppings of choice (e.g., coarse sea salt, dairy or nondairy grated cheese, sesame, or poppy seeds)

▸ Preheat the oven to 350°F (static) or 325°F (convection).

▸ In a large bowl, whisk together the dry ingredients except the yeast. Cut the shortening into small pieces and cut into the dry ingredients with a dough paddle attachment on a stand electric mixer or a pastry cutter by hand.

▸ In a smaller bowl, stir together the liquid ingredients until combined. Slowly add liquid mixture to the dry ingredient bowl, mixing until fully incorporated. Pour in the yeast and beat an additional minute thereafter to fully integrate the yeast granules.

DINNER ROLLS:

▸ Oil 12 muffin cups and scoop dough evenly into the cups, smoothing the tops as much as possible with a rubber spatula. Brush with milk, egg white, or oil.

▸ Sprinkle with any toppings you choose and bake for 12–15 minutes, until the tops are lightly browned, the dough has risen, and it doesn't sink when touched with a finger. Remove to cool until ready to serve.

continues

CLOVERLEAF OR PULL-APART ROLLS:

▸ Prepare popover trays by spraying with oil. Separate the dough into approximately 20 equal-size balls and dip each ball into the melted butter or nondairy alternative. Drop two or three butter-dipped balls into each popover cup.

▸ Sprinkle the tops with your favorite toppings and bake for approximately 12 minutes, or until the tops are lightly browned, the dough has approximately doubled in size, and it springs back to the touch.

BREADSTICKS:

▸ Lightly dust a clean counter or pastry mat with Jules Gluten Free All Purpose Flour. Scoop out approximately 6 balls of dough and gently roll each to a bread stick shape, then place on a parchment-lined baking sheet.

▸ Brush the tops with beaten egg white, milk, or olive oil, then sprinkle with any toppings you choose and bake for 12–15 minutes, until the tops are lightly browned, the dough has risen, and it doesn't sink when touched with a finger. Remove from the oven to cool until ready to serve.

MAKES 12 DINNER ROLLS OR 8–10 BREADSTICKS

Focaccia

Your guests will think they've died and gone to Italy. I'd like to say there's a mystique to this exquisite treat, but, alas, it's downright simple. Viva Italia!

1½ cups Jules Gluten Free All Purpose Flour (pages 6, 8)

¼ teaspoon oregano

Pinch or two of garlic powder

½ teaspoon kosher or sea salt

2 egg whites or egg substitute of choice (like one recipe of Egg Substitute #1 or 7, pages 15, 16)

2 tablespoons extra-virgin olive oil

½ teaspoon apple cider vinegar

⅔ cup unflavored liquid creamer, warmed (dairy or nondairy)

2¼ teaspoons (1 packet) rapid rise or bread machine yeast, gluten-free

2 sprigs of fresh rosemary, chopped, and/or coarse sea salt for topping

▸ Whisk together all the dry ingredients except the yeast. Combine the wet ingredients and blend, reserving some of the creamer. Using a stand mixer set to low, gradually add the dry ingredients plus the yeast. Add more creamer as needed to yield a firm but sticky dough that can still be spread. Beat on high for 3 minutes.

▸ Prepare a pizza pan (a crisper style pan with lots of holes is best) by covering it with aluminum foil and spraying lightly with cooking oil. Spoon the dough onto the prepared pan and coat your hands well with olive oil. Spread the dough out with the palms of your hands and shape it into a square—spread more thinly for a sandwich thickness or more thickly to achieve a higher rise. Cover lightly with oiled wax paper and set aside to rise for 10 minutes in a warming drawer or oven preheated to 200°F and turned off.

▸ Preheat the oven to 375°F. Remove the cover from the bread, brush the bread with olive oil, and sprinkle with fresh rosemary and/or salt, return to the preheated oven, and bake for about 25 minutes, until golden brown but not crispy.

▸ Cooking time will vary depending on your pan.

▸ Serve as is, or top with buffalo mozzarella, fresh tomatoes, balsamic vinegar, olive oil and basil, pesto, sliced olives, or hummus.

SERVES 6–8

Hamburger and Hot Dog Buns

Yes, people actually make their own hamburger and hot dog buns . . . they don't have to be spit out of a machine! And you can control what goes into them this way. Pass the mustard!

3 large eggs, room temperature or egg substitute of choice
(like Egg Substitute #1 or 7, pages 15, 16)
3 tablespoons extra-virgin olive oil
2 tablespoons honey or agave nectar (omit if using ginger ale)
2¾ cups Jules Gluten Free All Purpose Flour (pages 6, 8)
¼ cup nondairy milk powder or buttermilk powder
1 teaspoon salt
1 tablespoon granulated cane sugar
10 ounces sparkling water, club soda, ginger ale, or gluten-free ale
2¼ teaspoons (1 packet) rapid rise or bread machine yeast, gluten-free
Extra olive oil and milk (dairy or nondairy) for brushing on rolls
Sesame seeds, poppy seeds, or other topping of choice

▸ Prepare English muffin or bun pans by oiling lightly with olive oil or canola oil spray. Place the rings on a parchment-lined baking sheet and set aside. You may also shape these buns by hand; in that case, simply line a baking sheet with parchment paper and set aside.

▸ In a large mixing bowl, whisk together the eggs, oil, and honey.

▸ In another large bowl, whisk all the dry ingredients except the yeast (flour, milk powder, salt, and sugar). With the mixer on low speed, slowly pour the dry ingredients into the liquids to combine. Continue beating while slowly pouring the carbonated liquid into the mix. When incorporated, add the yeast. Beat until the batter is smooth, then increase mixing speed and beat for 4 minutes. The batter will be wet.

▸ Pour the batter into oiled ring pans, filling no more than halfway up. If not using pans or rings, you may dollop batter onto parchment paper or shape by hand by preparing a clean counter or pastry mat dusted with plenty of gluten-free flour or cornstarch (the dough is very wet). Divide the dough into 9–10 equal parts and individually pat out into a bun shape by rolling in the flour. Don't make the buns too large at this stage, unless you're looking for kaiser rolls! Place on a parchment-lined baking sheet. Brush all buns lightly with olive oil.

continues

▸ Cover with oiled wax paper and let rise in a warm, moist place for 30 minutes (an oven preheated to 200°F, then turned off, with a bowl of water in the oven to add moisture, is a good option). Do not let the rolls rise to more than double their size, or they will rise too much to support themselves and will collapse when cooling.

▸ When the bread has risen, lightly brush with milk to help the buns brown and sprinkle any toppings on at this point.

▸ Preheat the oven to 375°F (static) or 350°F (convection) and bake the buns uncovered for 20–25 minutes. The rolls should have risen above the tops of the pans, and will be golden brown with a nice crust. Remove to cool in the pans for 5 minutes, then gently remove from the pans and serve with your favorite burger or dog!

MAKES APPROXIMATELY 10 BUNS

Irish Soda Bread
(a.k.a. Treacle Tea Cake)

Typical Irish soda bread does not contain fruit, nor is it very sweet; which, in my opinion, leaves it a bit dry. Breakfast soda breads—or those offered at tea—often are the opposite, owing their moistness to "treacle," or molasses and added fruit (I used baking raisins; sultanas would be a nice option, too). The result: an Irish soda bread that is definitely not dry or crumbly.

3¼ cups Jules Gluten Free All Purpose Flour (pages 6, 8)

¼ cup flaxseed meal

½ teaspoon fine sea salt

½ teaspoon coarse sea salt

2 teaspoons baking soda

1 teaspoon baking powder, gluten-free

1 teaspoon granulated cane sugar

¼ teaspoon ginger

¼ teaspoon cardamom

2 tablespoons dark molasses (e.g., blackstrap molasses)

½ teaspoon apple cider vinegar

1 cup vanilla yogurt (dairy or nondairy)

¾ cup gluten-free beer, ginger ale, club soda, or Perrier

½ cup baking raisins or sultanas (or boil raisins in water, drain, then add to the recipe)

olive oil or milk (dairy or nondairy) for top

▸ Preheat the oven to 400°F (static) or 375°F (convection, preferred).

▸ In a large mixing bowl, use a pastry cutter or large slotted spoon and mix all the dry ingredients together thoroughly. Add the molasses, vinegar, and yogurt, stirring together until the dough is raggedy and dry, but mixed. Gradually add the beer and raisins, squishing the dough together with your hands until it will hold together in a ball shape.

▸ Roll the ball in a light coating of gluten-free flour and place onto a parchment-lined baking sheet. Press the dough down slightly to make a dome, rather than a ball. Using a sharp knife, make a crisscross cut into the top of the dome, cutting down approximately ½ inch without pulling the dough. Brush the dough with olive oil or milk of choice.

▸ Place in preheated oven for 10 minutes, then reduce heat to 325°F for 25–35 minutes, until cooked through (knock on the bottom, listening for a hollow sound).

▸ Remove from the oven when cooked through and wrap in a tea towel to cool. The towel will help to keep the bread moist and soften the crust a bit.

MAKES 1 LOAF

Pizza Dough

I've seen folks who have been deprived of real pizza for so long tear up when they finally taste their first safe and normal pizza.

You and everyone else will love this recipe. I recommend using a pizza crisper tray. They are usually circular pans and have lots of little holes in them to help the air flow and to make the outside of the crust crisper, while allowing the inside crust to remain chewy. I also love using portable pizza ovens like the Presto Pizzazz Pizza Oven. This handy gadget is fun to watch in action and takes any guesswork out of rising and baking a pizza. Either way, this recipe will make a thin or thick crust—whichever you prefer—and will make your whole family happy.

1½ cups Jules Gluten Free All Purpose Flour (pages 6, 8)

¼ teaspoon oregano

Pinch or two of garlic powder

½ teaspoon salt

2 egg whites or egg substitute of choice (like one recipe of Egg Substitute #1 or 7, pages 15, 16), room temperature

2 tablespoons extra-virgin olive oil

½ teaspoon apple cider vinegar

⅔ cup liquid creamer (dairy or nondairy), warmed, or ½ cup warm water plus 3 tablespoons milk powder (dairy or nondairy)

2¼ teaspoons (1 packet) rapid rise yeast, gluten-free

Additional olive oil to brush onto the crust

▸ Whisk together dry ingredients except yeast; set aside. In a large mixing bowl, combine egg whites, olive oil, cider vinegar, and ⅓ cup creamer (or ¼ cup water plus milk powder alternative). Using a stand mixer (preferably), turn to the low setting and slowly add in the dry ingredient mix. Gradually add in the remaining creamer or water to get a firm but very sticky dough that can still be spread. Pour in the yeast and beat on high for an additional 3 minutes.

▸ Cover a pizza pan or baking sheet with aluminum foil and lightly oil the foil. Spoon the dough into the middle of the pan and pour olive oil into your hands so that the dough won't stick to them when you can shape it. Spread the dough into a 12-inch circle. Leave a raised outer edge so the pizza sauce won't spill out.

continues

▸ Cover with oiled waxed paper and let the crust rise about 10 minutes in a warm spot like a warming drawer or oven preheated to 200°F and turned off.

▸ After rising, preheat the oven to 375°F (static). Poke holes in the crust with a fork, then bake for approximately 15 minutes. The cooking time will vary depending on your pan, but the crust should have risen nicely by this time and just begun to slightly brown.

▸ Lightly brush olive oil onto the crust edges. Spread with pizza or marinara sauce (see recipe, page 167) and your toppings of choice and cook until the cheese is bubbly. If you add vegetable toppings, I find they taste best if you sauté them in olive oil before adding them to the crust.

▸ Note: You may par-bake the crust, freeze, and bake for later use. If doing so, stop baking after the first 15 minute bake cycle, fully cool, then wrap in foil and freeze for later use. Remove from the freezer when ready to use, preheat the oven to 375°F, spread sauce and toppings, then bake for 15–20 minutes, or until the cheese is bubbling.

See photo insert.

Popcorn Bread

Popcorn flour is a fun, gluten-free alternative but is not available in any store (that I know of!). To make it, simply pop your favorite popping corn, then put it in a food processor or blender and grind it to a fine powder—voilà!—popcorn flour. The resulting flour imparts a distinctive popcorn flavor. In this bread, it also offers the benefits of another whole-grain flour but is too airy to support a loaf of bread on its own, so must be combined with other gluten-free flours that offer bulk as well. A really unique treat that is fun to make and to eat!

1 cup popcorn flour

½ cup gluten-free oat flour or gluten-free oats ground into flour (or brown rice flour)

2 eggs, lightly beaten or egg substitute of choice (like Egg Substitute #1 or 2, page 15)

2 tablespoons flaxseed meal

6 tablespoons hot water

1 cup Jules Gluten Free All Purpose Flour (pages 6, 8)

¾ cup buckwheat flour

⅔ cup powdered milk (dairy or nondairy) or buttermilk powder

½ teaspoon baking soda

2 teaspoons baking powder, gluten-free

1 teaspoon sea salt

1 cup vanilla yogurt (dairy or nondairy)

1 teaspoon apple cider vinegar

3 tablespoons extra-virgin olive oil

3 tablespoons honey or light agave nectar

2¼ teaspoons (1 packet) rapid rise yeast, gluten-free

Sesame seeds, sea salt, or poppy seeds (optional toppings)

BREAD MACHINE DIRECTIONS:

▸ Grind the popcorn and oats (if using gluten-free oats instead of already ground gluten-free oat flour) in a food processor until fine. Use a small bowl food processor or blender, as the popcorn is very light and will float away from the blade if given too much room in the bowl.

▸ Stir the eggs with a fork in a small bowl to mix the yolks and whites together. Add flaxseed meal to hot water in a separate bowl and set aside to steep for 10–15 minutes, or until viscous. Gather all the other ingredients and plug in the bread machine, inserting the pan and paddle attachment.

▸ Sift dry ingredients (except yeast) together in a large bowl and set aside.

continues

‣ Add all the liquid ingredients to the bread machine pan first. Add the dry ingredients next and make a well in the center for the yeast. Add the yeast last and set the machine to the gluten-free setting or a setting with only one rise cycle and no punch-down.

‣ During the knead cycle periodically check to see that the dry ingredients have been fully integrated into the dough, scraping down the sides with a rubber spatula if necessary. Add any toppings like sesame seeds, sea salt, poppy seeds, and so on at the conclusion of the knead cycle. Check to be sure the internal temperature of the loaf has reached 205–210°F before removing the pan when the baking is completed. If necessary, add baking time on the machine or place the pan in a 350°F (static) oven and check at 5-minute intervals to determine when it is fully cooked. Remove the bread to a cooling rack for 15 minutes, then gently remove the bread from the pan and slice when fully cooled.

OVEN DIRECTIONS:

‣ Grind the popcorn and oats (if using gluten-free oats instead of already ground gluten-free oat flour) in a food processor until fine. Use a small bowl food processor or blender, as the popcorn is very light and will float away from the blade if given too much room in the bowl.

‣ Add flaxseed meal to hot water and set aside to steep for 10–15 minutes, or until viscous. Sift dry ingredients (except yeast) together in a large bowl and set aside. When the flaxseed meal is viscous, pour it into a large mixing bowl along with the eggs, yogurt, cider vinegar, olive oil, and honey. Beat until well mixed.

‣ Gradually stir in the dry ingredients and beat until incorporated. Add the yeast last and beat an additional 2–3 minutes, to ensure that the yeast is fully mixed into the dough.

‣ Scoop the dough into an oiled 9 x 5-inch loaf pan. Add any toppings like sesame seeds, sea salt, or poppy seeds at this point, then spray waxed paper with cooking oil or dampen a cloth and cover the loaf, setting it aside to rise in a warm place like a warming drawer or an oven preheated to 200°F and turned off. Let the bread rise for 30 minutes or until the bread has risen to just above the top of the pan, then bake in an oven preheated to 350°F (static) or 325°F (convection). Bake for 30–35 minutes, or until a toothpick inserted into the center comes out clean, the loaf sounds hollow when thumped, and an instant-read thermometer inserted into the center of the bread reads 205°F.

‣ Remove to a wire rack to cool for 10–15 minutes, then remove from the pan to cool completely before cutting. Store in a zip-top bag to retain freshness.

MAKES 1 LOAF

Soft Pretzels

This recipe is one of my cooking class favorites. Soft pretzels seem like they must be difficult, but the trick is really in the very simple soda bath. Don't be daunted . . . I've had many, many first-timers tell me of their successes with this recipe. Yours is less than an hour away!

⅓ cup warm water (110°F)

1 teaspoon granulated cane sugar

2¼ teaspoons (1 packet) active dry yeast, gluten-free

1⅓ cups plus 2 tablespoons Jules Gluten Free All Purpose Flour
   (pages 6, 8)

½ teaspoon salt

1 egg or egg substitute of choice (like Egg Substitute #1 or 2, page 15)

1 tablespoon honey or agave nectar

Canola or extra-virgin olive oil for brushing on top of pretzels

⅔ cup baking soda for soda bath

Butter or nondairy alternative for brushing on top of pretzels

Coarse sea salt, sesame seeds, or other toppings of choice

▸ In a large mixing bowl, mix warm water, sugar, and yeast and let stand for 5 minutes. Whisk the flour and salt and set aside.

▸ In a large bowl, whisk together the egg and honey. Stir in the proofed yeast mixture, then add half the flour to this wet mixture bowl. Beat on the low speed of an electric mixer for 1 minute, or until well blended. Add in the remaining flour and blend until incorporated. If the dough is dry, add ½ to 1 teaspoon more warm water and mix well. The dough should hold together without being sticky.

▸ Pull apart six equal-size dough balls. Gently roll each ball to approximately ¾-inch-diameter logs. Take both ends of each log and twist into the middle, pressing together to form a pretzel shape using gluten-free flour to dust the rolling surface, only as necessary. Gently dab water under each of the ends of the twist to help them stick together, or they will release during the boil.

▸ Lay each pretzel onto a parchment-paper lined baking sheet. Use a pastry brush to dust off any excess flour, then liberally brush the pretzels with canola or olive oil. Cover with a damp cloth or oiled wax paper and proof for 30 minutes in a warm place like a warming drawer or an oven preheated to 200°F, then turned off.

continues

▸ Prepare a soda bath by adding ⅔ cup baking soda to 10 cups of water in a large pot and bring to a boil over high heat. Stir until the soda is completely dissolved.

▸ Preheat the oven to 375°F (static) or 350°F (convection).

▸ Once the soda bath has achieved a rolling boil, gently submerge pretzels individually into the bath for 25 seconds, flipping over after about 15 seconds. Remove with a slotted spoon or skimmer, drain, and replacc the pretzels onto the parchment-lined baking sheet.

▸ Brush the pretzels with melted butter or nondairy alternative and top with coarse sea salt or other toppings. Bake uncovered for 10 to 15 minutes, or until light golden brown. Do not overbake.

MAKES APPROXIMATELY 6 TRADITIONALLY SIZED PRETZELS

Sandwich Bread

This recipe boasts nutritious grains like flaxseed meal, which contributes dietary fiber and other beneficial nutritional properties like high omega-3 fatty acids. The simple addition of even just two tablespoons of flaxseed meal to this bread adds 4 grams of dietary fiber and 3 grams of protein.

While I love using yogurt as an ingredient in my breads—it keeps the crumb nice and moist for days—it is a variable in baking, as low fat, fat-free, soy, rice, and coconut all have different moisture levels and viscosities. So the directions indicate the minimum amount of yogurt recommended for this recipe; depending on the type of yogurt used, a small amount of extra yogurt may be needed to thin this thick dough to the consistency needed to spread out in a pan to form a nice loaf.

> 3 cups Jules Gluten Free All Purpose Flour (pages 6, 8)
> ¼ cup flaxseed meal, buckwheat flour, brown rice flour, or a combination of these
> ¼ cup dry milk powder (dairy or nondairy)
> ½ teaspoon baking soda
> 2 teaspoons baking powder, gluten-free
> 1 teaspoon sea salt
> 2 tablespoons honey or agave nectar
> 1¼ cup vanilla yogurt (dairy or nondairy)
> 1 teaspoon apple cider vinegar
> ¼ cup extra-virgin olive oil
> 2 eggs or egg substitute of choice (like Egg Substitute #7, page 16)
> 1 tablespoon rapid rise or bread machine yeast, gluten-free
> 1 teaspoon granulated cane sugar
> 1 tablespoon flax seeds or sesame seeds (optional topping)
> 1 tablespoon coarse sea salt (optional topping)

STAND MIXER AND OVEN BAKING

▸ Whisk these dry ingredients together in a large bowl: flours, milk powder, baking soda, baking powder, and salt.

continues

- In the large mixing bowl of a stand mixer, stir together the remaining liquid ingredients (honey, yogurt, apple cider vinegar, oil, and eggs). Gradually add the dry ingredients in with the wet by pouring slowly into the wet bowl while mixing with the paddle attachment. Once incorporated, add the yeast granules and sugar and beat well—1–2 more minutes.

- The dough will be very thick (much more like regular wheat flour bread dough than you may be used to with gluten-free); however, if the dough seems too thick to spread into a loaf pan, gradually mix in more yogurt, 1 tablespoon at a time, until the dough is still thick, but able to be smoothed with a spatula.

- Scoop the dough into an oiled bread pan (use a dark metal pan if you like a darker crust on your bread; lighter, shiny metal or glass if you like a light crust). Use a 9 x 5 x 3-inch loaf pan; if using a smaller pan, lower the oven temperature by 25 degrees and expect to bake the loaf longer before being totally cooked in the middle.

- Smooth the top, sprinkle with any toppings, then cover with a damp towel or a sheet of wax paper sprayed with cooking oil. Set the covered dough for at least 30 minutes in a warm place like an oven warming drawer or an oven preheated to 200°F then turned off. It should rise at least to the top of the pan before baking.

- Remove the cover from the raised dough and transfer to a preheated convection oven set to 275°F or a preheated static oven set to 300°F. Cook for approximately 60 minutes, or until the crust is browning nicely and a cake tester or skewer inserted into the center of the loaf comes out clean (internal temperature should reach 205–210°F). Remove to a cooling rack. When cooled for 15 minutes, gently remove from the loaf pan to finish cooling before slicing.

BREAD MACHINE DIRECTIONS

- When using a bread machine, always be sure to add all liquid ingredients to the pan first, followed by the dry ingredients. Whisk together the yolks and whites before adding to the bread machine with the other liquids; alternatively, allow the flaxseed meal egg substitute to steep in water for 10–15 minutes before adding. Bring all liquids to room temperature before adding to the machine, if possible.

- I recommend sifting all dry ingredients together in a bowl first, then pouring the mixture into the bread machine pan after all the liquids are added. Reserve the yeast for last in bread machines, making a small well in the top of the dry ingredients in the pan, and pouring the sugar, then the yeast into that well.

continues

▸ Select either the gluten-free bread setting on your machine or the setting with only one rise cycle and no punch-down (2-pound loaf setting).

▸ Once the ingredients have mixed, the dough will be very thick (much more like regular wheat flour bread dough than you may be used to with gluten-free); however, if the dough seems too thick as it is mixing in this recipe, gradually add more yogurt, 1 tablespoon at a time while the bread machine is mixing, until the dough is still very thick, but able to be smoothed with a spatula. Be sure to check the bread with a spatula throughout the mixing process to ensure that all the dry ingredients have been incorporated.

▸ When the machine is done mixing, smooth the top with a rubber spatula and sprinkle any desired toppings on top of the loaf.

▸ Test the temperature of the interior of the loaf before removing from the pan—it should have reached approximately 205–210°F. If it hasn't yet reached that temperature, either add time to your bread machine as another bake cycle or simply put the pan into a regular oven at 350°F (static), testing the temperature again at 5-minute intervals.

▸ Once a cake tester or skewer inserted into the center of the loaf comes out clean and the internal temperature reaches 205–210°F, remove to a cooling rack. When cooled for 15 minutes, gently remove from the loaf pan to finish cooling before slicing.

MAKES 1 LOAF

See photo insert.

Sweet Potato Biscuits

They're beautiful. They smell divine. And they pack the nutritional punch of sweet potatoes! Trifecta!

> 1 teaspoon lemon juice
> ½ cup milk (dairy or nondairy)
> 1 cup Jules Gluten Free All Purpose Flour (pages 6, 8)
> 1¼ teaspoons fine sea salt
> 1 tablespoon plus 1 teaspoon baking powder, gluten-free
> 4 tablespoons cold shortening
> 1 cup sweet potatoes, cooked, peeled, and mashed
> Butter or nondairy alternative for tops of biscuits

▸ Preheat the oven to 375°F (static) or 350°F (convection).

▸ Add the lemon juice to ½ cup of milk and set aside (this creates a buttermilk substitute).

▸ In a medium-size bowl, whisk together all dry ingredients. Cut the shortening into the dry mix using a pastry cutter or in a food processor until the mixture is crumbly. Add the cooked, mashed sweet potatoes and stir until blended. Slowly add the buttermilk mixture and stir with a large fork until a well-mixed, fluffy dough is formed.

▸ Turn the dough out onto a clean surface dusted with gluten-free flour or cornstarch. Dust your hands as well. Form a ball with the dough and then flatten with your hands to ½–¾-inch thick. Use a biscuit or cookie cutter to cut the biscuits (cut straight down, do not twist with the cutter) and lay them onto a parchment-lined baking sheet.

▸ Place a small pat of butter or nondairy alternative on top of the biscuits and bake for 15–18 minutes or until the tops are lightly browned (do not overbake!).

SERVES 6

Flour Tortillas

Simple, as they should be. Make a bunch while you're at it. Tortillas are back on your menu!

2 cups Jules Gluten Free All Purpose Flour (pages 6, 8)
¾ teaspoon sea salt
4 tablespoons shortening
²/₃–1 cup very warm water

▸ Combine the flour, salt, and shortening in a food processor, pulsing until it is evenly distributed and is a fine meal consistency. Turning the food processor back on, slowly pour ⅔ cup of water through the feeding tube until the dough forms a nice ball. You may need slightly more water to achieve this consistency.

▸ Divide and roll the dough into 8 equal-size discs. Set aside on a plate and wrap in clear plastic wrap.

▸ Let the dough sit for approximately 30 minutes. Meanwhile, prepare your filling for fajitas, burritos, soft tacos, sandwiches, or whatever you prefer (see Fish Tacos recipe, page 149, or Sweet Potato and Black Bean Burritos, page 164).

▸ Preheat a griddle or large skillet to medium-high heat (do not oil the surface).

▸ Take each ball individually and flatten slightly. On a clean surface or pastry mat lightly dusted with gluten-free flour, roll the individual tortillas. This dough is capable of being rolled extremely thin without breaking, but it should only be rolled to the thickness of a traditional flour tortilla to prevent the edges from crisping and cracking when you prepare the tortillas. Roll in different directions to make the tortillas round. If the edges are uneven once rolled, simply lay a paper plate gently on top for a template and cut around it to form even edges.

continues

▸ Lift each tortilla gently using your rolling pin or a spatula to transfer the tortillas one at a time to the hot cooking surface. You will only be cooking the tortillas for a very short time, so watch for when the tortilla starts to bubble with air, then flip to the other side to cook for a few seconds only—cook less than you would think you need. It doesn't hurt to overcook the tortillas slightly, but the edges will become crispy and make rolling a bit more challenging.

▸ When done, place tortillas on a towel-lined plate and wrap each in layers of the towel until ready to serve; if serving much later, seal the tortillas with wax paper separating each one inside a zip top bag once fully cooled. Refrigerate or freeze. To reheat later, wrap in a towel and microwave briefly on medium-low heat.

MAKES 8 TORTILLAS

Whole-Grain
Sandwich Bread—Yeast-Free

I love sharing this recipe with folks who are particularly apprehensive about baking with yeast. This recipe solves that problem, is ready within the hour, and offers super whole-grain goodness to those of us searching for more nutrition in our diets. I have suggested a number of different gluten-free grains here, but feel free to simply substitute with other whole-grain gluten-free flours rather than starches that you have on hand, understanding that any substitution will change not only the nutritional profile of the bread, but also the flavor and texture as well.

Enjoy this wholesome bread that is easily made and baked within one hour! Whether or not you avoid yeast, you won't miss it in this bread that is sure to become one of your favorites!

1 cup Jules Gluten Free All Purpose Flour
½ cup buckwheat flour
¼ cup millet flour
¼ cup flaxseed meal
¼ cup certified gluten-free oats
⅛ cup certified gluten-free oat flour
⅛ cup teff
1 teaspoon sea salt
1½ teaspoons baking powder, gluten-free

½ teaspoon baking soda
3 eggs or egg substitute of choice (like Egg Substitute #1, 2, and 7, pages 15–16)
1 tablespoon agave nectar or honey
1 teaspoon apple cider vinegar
⅔ cup vanilla yogurt (dairy or nondairy)
¼ cup sparkling water or other carbonated liquid (e.g., Perrier, club soda, or ginger ale)
½ cup sunflower seeds

▶ Preheat oven to 350°F (static) or 325°F (convection).

▶ Whisk together all the dry ingredients in a large bowl and set aside.

▶ Beat the eggs until frothy, then add the remaining wet ingredients and blend well. Slowly mix the dry ingredients in with the wet, and stir until thoroughly incorporated. Mix in the seeds last.

▶ Scoop the dough into an oiled, 9 x 5-inch metal loaf pan and sprinkle with any toppings of choice. Bake for 35 minutes, or until a toothpick inserted into the center comes out clean, a nice crust has formed, and the internal temperature is approximately 190°F.

▶ Remove to cool on a wire rack for 5–10 minutes, then remove to finish cooling before slicing.

See photo insert.

4

Soups

Butternut Squash Soup

It's officially Fall when I make up my first batch of this family favorite. Venture out from here and add other ingredients you like. It's soup—you can't go wrong.

2 tablespoons extra-virgin olive oil

1 medium onion, peeled and diced

1 chile pepper, seeded and diced, or 2–3 small chipotle chiles, chopped (optional)

Leaves from 1–2 fresh rosemary sprigs or 1 teaspoon dried rosemary

2 medium butternut squash (about 3 pounds), peeled, seeded, and quartered

6–7 cups vegetable stock, gluten-free

Salt and pepper to taste

▸ Heat the olive oil in a medium pot and add the onions and chiles (if using), stirring until the onions are softened. Add the rosemary and squash to the onion mixture. Pour in enough stock to just cover the squash. Bring to a boil, then lower to a simmer and cook, uncovered, until the squash is fork tender (30–40 minutes); some of the liquid will cook off during this process.

▸ Remove from the heat and, when cool, use a large food processor or a handheld stick blender to puree the mixture until smooth. Add salt and pepper to taste. Serve warm.

SERVES 4

Wintry Chili

There are entire books written about chili. Do you have your own favorite recipe? If not, start here. Then spice it up, spice it down, vegetarian-ize it, add more beans . . . you get the idea. Makes you pine for cold weather and a football game, doesn't it?

2 tablespoons extra-virgin olive oil

14 ounces firm tofu, pressed between two paper towels and diced, or 2 cups chicken or ground beef, diced

¼ cup diced onions

1 (4-ounce) can diced green chiles

1 tablespoon chili powder

7 cups diced fresh tomatoes, or two 28-ounce cans diced tomatoes

2 cups tomato juice

1 (15-ounce) can black beans, rinsed

2 (15-ounce) cans light red kidney beans, rinsed

1 (15-ounce) can Great Northern beans, rinsed

1 (35-ounce) can dark red kidney beans, rinsed

2 cups cooked corn kernels or 1 can, rinsed

4 teaspoons dried oregano

3 tablespoons chili powder

2 teaspoons allspice

1 tablespoon cinnamon

1 teaspoon cumin

1 teaspoon ground cloves

1½ teaspoons crushed red pepper

1 tablespoon chili paste (omit if you don't like a lot of spice)

2 teaspoons lime juice

½ cup crushed peanuts (optional; omit if making nut-free)

▸ In a large skillet, heat the olive oil over medium-high heat. Add the tofu or meat and sauté just until cooked through, then add the onions, green chiles, and 1 tablespoon chili powder. When fully cooked, stir in the tomatoes and tomato juice. Turn the flame down to low.

▸ In a large stock pot or soup pot, combine all the remaining ingredients except the peanuts. Heat to medium and add the tofu or meat mixture. Stir and cover, cooking until the liquid has cooked down to the consistency you prefer. Sprinkle with crushed peanuts when serving, if desired.

▸ This pot will serve your family for days to come! Spoon over cornbread or rice, or enjoy on its own—it's sure to warm you this winter!

SERVES 10

Curried Carrot Soup

I love curry. There, I said it. And it's so much fun to add different things to this curried soup, like these sweet carrots. It'll warm you from the inside. Beautiful, simple, nutritious—soup *is* good food.

1 large onion, chopped

3 tablespoons extra-virgin olive oil

1½ tablespoons Thai yellow curry paste

2 teaspoons curry powder

¼ teaspoon red pepper flakes

½ tablespoon peeled and finely chopped fresh ginger

1 clove garlic, finely chopped

2 pounds carrots, peeled and chopped

¾ cup apple cider

½ cup vegetable stock, gluten-free

1 (14-ounce) can unsweetened coconut milk

1 tablespoon red wine or balsamic vinegar

4 cilantro stems, stripped of leaves and chopped
    (reserve leaves for garnish)

GARNISH:

8 tablespoons sweet, not hot, chutney of choice (optional)

Leaves from 4 sprigs cilantro

Fresh ginger, peeled and sliced into thin circles, about 1½ tablespoons

⅓ cup sliced almonds, toasted (optional)

3 tablespoons chopped chives (optional)

▸ Add all the ingredients except the garnishes to a large pot and bring to a boil. Once boiling, reduce the heat to medium-low and cover, stirring periodically until ready to serve, at least 30 minutes.

▸ Spoon 1 tablespoon of chutney, if using, into each bowl. Top with soup then add remaining garnish ingredients. Serve warm.

SERVES 8

Gazpacho

This chilled soup is a wonderfully crunchy and refreshing dish to serve any time of year. Follow the instructions to puree vegetables and form the liquid soup base, then add chunks of vegetables to preserve the crisp texture of this soup. Croutons (see page 77) are a wonderful garnish as well.

> 6–7 green onions, diced
>
> 1 cucumber, peeled and diced
>
> 1 green pepper, diced
>
> 1 red pepper, diced
>
> 1 (28-ounce) can peeled whole tomatoes (discard juice from the can) or approximately 10 fresh tomatoes of choice, peeled
>
> 1 stalk celery, diced (tops included)
>
> 1 (28-ounce) can diced tomatoes or approximately 10 fresh tomatoes of choice, diced
>
> 2 cans (11-ounces total) V8 juice
>
> 1 tablespoon lemon juice
>
> ⅛ teaspoon minced garlic
>
> 2–3 teaspoons Tabasco, or to taste
>
> ½ tablespoon Lea & Perrins Worcestershire Sauce
>
> Fresh cilantro to taste (optional)

▸ In a large food processor or blender, combine half of the green onions, half of the cucumber, half of the green and red peppers, and all of the peeled whole tomatoes. Blend until pureed. Pour into a large bowl or pitcher. Add the celery and the other remaining veggies, V8 juice, lemon juice, garlic, Tabasco, and Worcestershire sauce, to taste. Stir, cover, and chill in the refrigerator until serving.

▸ Once chilled, serve with fresh cilantro and gluten-free Croutons (see page 77).

SERVES 6

Lentil Soup

Lentils, cumin, curry, coconut milk . . . this sounds like Indian food! And it is, which means it's stick-to-your-ribs good and fills the kitchen with its essence. Dial back the curry if you don't think you like Indian food. The protein-rich lentils are healthful enough to warrant fine-tuning this soup to your tastes.

1 onion, finely chopped

2 teaspoons extra-virgin olive oil

2 tablespoons hot curry paste

1 tablespoon peeled and finely chopped fresh ginger root

1 teaspoon cumin

2 cups dried red lentils

6 cups vegetable stock, gluten-free

1 (14-ounce) can coconut milk

Juice and zest of 1 lime

Salt and pepper to taste

2 tablespoons chopped fresh mint (optional)

▸ Sauté the onions and olive oil in a large pan until transparent. Add the curry paste, ginger, and cumin, stirring gently for 3 minutes.

▸ Add the lentils and stock. Bring to a boil, then reduce the heat to a simmer and cook for 20 minutes.

▸ Add the coconut milk and cook for another 10 minutes. Just before serving, add the lime zest and juice, salt and pepper, and chopped mint.

SERVES 4–6

Mexican Stew (Sancocho)

Three kids I know, who swear they don't like sweet potatoes, each had seconds and thirds of this sweet potato–based soup. There's something about the combination of ingredients here that is universally appealing.

> 4 cups water
> 1 teaspoon salt
> ¼ cup chopped fresh cilantro or 1 tablespoon dried cilantro
> 1 ripe plantain, peeled and cut into 1-inch pieces (optional)
> 1 large yellow onion, diced
> 2 pounds sweet potatoes, peeled and cut into 1-inch pieces
> 1 ear of corn, husked and cut into 2-inch pieces
> ½ cup diced red, orange, or yellow peppers
> 1 tablespoon canola oil
> 1 teaspoon ground cumin
> 1 teaspoon ground coriander seed
> ½ teaspoon paprika
> 1 package Sazón Goya seasoning or 2 teaspoons Konriko Chipotle Seasoning (MSG-free)
> 1 pound tomatoes, chopped
> 2 (15-ounce) cans black beans, rinsed and drained

▸ Pour the water into a slow cooker or large pot and add the salt, cilantro, plantain, half of the onions, and all of the sweet potatoes and corn. If using a large pot, bring to a boil and cook over medium heat until the potatoes are tender, at least 30 minutes. If using a slow cooker, cook on high heat for 2–3 hours, or low heat for 6 hours, just until the potatoes are tender.

▸ Meanwhile, sauté the remaining onions and the peppers in the canola oil in a medium skillet. Sauté until the onions are translucent, then add the remaining spices and seasoning, stirring to coat the onions and peppers. Stir in the tomatoes. Add to the stew together with the black beans when the potatoes are cooked to tender. Stir and heat the stew thoroughly.

▸ Spoon over cornbread (see recipe, page 107) or rice in bowls and serve warm.

SERVES 6–8

Pumpkin Soup

The two-line directions prove how simple this hearty, healthful soup is. Serve in your fine china to guests, or from a thermos on a Fall outing. It pleases, whatever the venue.

2 cups pumpkin puree or cooked, pureed butternut squash or cooked, pureed sweet potato
1 (14-ounce) can unsweetened coconut milk
1 (15-ounce) can cannelloni or navy beans, drained and rinsed
2 cups vegetable broth, gluten-free
1 teaspoon dried sage, crushed
1–2 tablespoons Thai yellow curry paste
Salt and pepper, to taste
Cracked black peppercorns to taste (as garnish)

▸ In medium saucepan combine pumpkin, coconut milk, beans, broth, and spices. Heat through.

▸ Season with salt and pepper. Sprinkle with cracked peppercorns.

SERVES 4

Vegetable Soup

One of my pet peeves with vegetable soup is that so many chefs prepare it with beef broth. While you may use beef broth in this soup, your vegetarian friends would appreciate it if you make truly *vegetarian* vegetable soup!

1 tablespoon garlic, diced

1 sweet onion, diced

1 tablespoon extra-virgin olive oil

1 pound baby carrots (1 small bag), sliced into chunks

1 cup diced celery stalks

8 cups vegetable broth, gluten-free

3 cups diced tomatoes (or one 28-ounce can)

2 cups diced potatoes, zucchini, or yellow squash

2 teaspoons dried oregano

2 cups cooked corn kernels (or one 16-ounce bag frozen corn)

1 (16-ounce) bag frozen peas

2 cups string beans (or one 16-ounce bag frozen string beans)

2 cups tomato sauce

Salt and black pepper, to taste

▸ In a large pot, sauté the garlic and onion in the olive oil until soft and translucent. Add the carrots and celery and continue sautéing until the celery begins to soften, about 3 more minutes.

▸ Add the broth, tomatoes, potatoes, and oregano and cook for about 15 minutes or until carrots are soft. Add the remaining vegetables and tomato sauce, cooking for another 15 minutes. If using softer vegetables like squash, add with only 5 minutes left of cooking so they retain some crunch. Add salt and pepper to taste before serving.

SERVES 6

Apple Pie, page 173

Banana Blueberry Muffins, page 37

Challah, page 105

Chocolate Chip Cookies, page 196

Chocolate Birthday Cake, page 176

Croutons, page 77

Crusty French Baguette, page 100

Lemon Bars, page 216

Buckeyes, page 185

Pancakes, page 60

Crustless Quiche, page 159

Pizza Dough, page 116

Sandwich Bread, page 122

Shortcakes, page 229

Traditional Stuffing, page 94

Tempura Vegetables, page 165

Whole-Grain Sandwich Bread—Yeast-Free, page 128

5

Main Events

Fried Catfish

Be sure to try this wonderful southern dish with Hushpuppies (see page 86)! Depending on how many catfish pieces you want to fry, your amounts will vary, but stick to the following proportions.

1 cup potato flakes or rice flakes, gluten-free
2 teaspoons salt
1 teaspoon black pepper, to taste
3 large eggs, stirred, or ¾ cup milk (dairy or nondairy)
½ cup yellow cornmeal
4 medium catfish fillets (5–6 ounces each), cleaned and skinned
Extra-virgin olive oil or other high heat cooking oil

▸ Prepare an electric skillet or large frying pan by covering the bottom with ¼ inch of oil and heating to medium-high.

▸ Arrange three flat-bottomed bowls in a row: the first bowl with the potato flakes, salt, and pepper; the next bowl with the stirred eggs or milk; the last bowl with the cornmeal.

▸ Wash the catfish pieces, pat dry, then dredge through the bowls in the given order and cook for 4 to 6 minutes on each side (it will depend on the size of each fillet). Cook until light golden brown on both sides and fish flakes easily with a fork. Drain on paper towels then place on a parchment-lined baking sheet in a warm oven until ready to serve.

SERVES 4

Grilled Chicken or Shrimp

Toss another shrimp on the barbie! But make sure your marinade is up to snuff. Here's the ticket . . . made with things you probably have in your pantry right now.

⅓ cup extra-virgin olive oil
Juice of one small lime (approximately 2 tablespoons)
½ teaspoon grated lime zest
2 cloves garlic, crushed (approximately 2 teaspoons)
1½ teaspoons fresh oregano (or 1 teaspoon dried oregano)
¼ teaspoon red pepper flakes
1 teaspoon salt
¼ teaspoon black pepper
1 tablespoon chili paste (optional)
1 pound boneless chicken breast, cut into 1–2 inch chunks *or* raw, peeled, and deveined shrimp

▸ Mix all the ingredients together in a large bowl, except the chicken or shrimp, to make the marinade. Toss the meat in the marinade and cover with plastic wrap; refrigerate until ready to cook.

▸ Grill approximately 2 minutes per side (chicken can take slightly longer) on a skewer or in a grill pan, or roast by placing the shrimp or chicken on an oiled baking sheet and drizzle with marinade. Spread out in a single layer to roast for 5 to 6 minutes, until the shrimp are pink or the chicken is white and cooked through; be careful not to overcook the shrimp, though, or it will become tough.

▸ Serve with rice or your favorite gluten-free pasta.

SERVES 4

Chicken Tenders (Fried Chicken)

Use white meat here for less fat and season according to your taste. It's way better than fast food and smells great in the kitchen!

1 pound chicken tenders or boneless chicken breast, butterflied
High heat canola oil for frying
¾ cup Jules Gluten Free All Purpose Flour (pages 6, 8)
2 large eggs, mixed, or ½ cup milk (dairy or nondairy)
1½ cups breadcrumbs, gluten-free (page 78)
½ teaspoon salt
¼ teaspoon pepper
½ teaspoon Italian seasoning or dried parsley (optional)

▸ Prepare the chicken by rinsing it with cold water then trimming off the fat. If using breasts, be sure to butterfly each piece. Set aside.

▸ In a large sauté pan, pour oil to approximately ⅓-inch deep and heat to medium-high.

▸ Meanwhile, arrange three plates or shallow bowls in a row: the first plate with the flour, the second plate with the mixed eggs or milk, and the third plate with breadcrumbs, salt, pepper, and seasoning. One piece at a time, dredge the chicken in flour, then cover with egg or milk, then dip into breadcrumbs. Add more flour, egg, or breadcrumbs to the bowls, as needed.

▸ Once the oil is hot (test by dropping some breadcrumbs in the oil—if it sizzles, it is ready), carefully lay the breaded chicken in the pan. Fry for 4 minutes then flip each piece and cook for an additional 4 minutes or until the meat reaches an internal temperature of 160°F. During cooking, the oil may become too hot and cook the pieces too quickly, so reduce the temperature as necessary.

▸ When fully cooked, remove the chicken and place on a paper towel–lined plate to absorb any excess oil.

▸ Serve hot or cold or use to make a scrumptious chicken parmesan (makes great leftovers, too)!

SERVES 4–6

Crab Cakes

As with any recipe, the best are made with the best ingredients. So, splurge for large lump crabmeat if you can—it makes all the difference in this recipe where all the focus should be on the crab, not the filler. If you're avoiding shellfish, seafood, or eggs, try the next recipe instead, Veggie "Crab" Cakes, for a great mock crab cake experience!

1½ pounds lump crabmeat (cleaned)

Approximately ¾ cup crushed corn tortilla chips, multigrain (gluten-free) chips like those from Food Should Taste Good, or gluten-free Chex cereal (rice or corn varieties)

⅛ cup minced red onions

⅓ cup chopped fresh parsley or Italian parsley

2 tablespoons fresh lemon juice

½ teaspoon dried mustard

1 teaspoon Tabasco

½ teaspoon salt

¼ teaspoon pepper

4 large eggs

Old Bay seasoning, to taste

Extra-virgin olive oil or other high heat oil for frying

▸ Combine all the ingredients, except the olive oil, in a medium-size mixing bowl and stir them together with a fork until fully incorporated. Stir gently so as not to break up the lump crabmeat more than necessary.

▸ Divide the crabmeat mixture into 8 equal portions and shape each portion into a patty.

FRYING:

▸ Heat the oil over medium-high heat in a large skillet. Place the patties into ¼ inch of hot oil and cook for 3 minutes on each side. Remove to drain on paper towel–lined plates and keep them in a warm oven until ready to serve.

BROILING:

▸ Heat the oil over medium-high heat in a large skillet. Flash fry each patty just until crisped on either side, then place them on a foil-lined cookie sheet and broil in the oven for another 5 minutes, flipping after 3 minutes. Be careful not to let the cakes burn!

SERVES 6–8

Veggie "Crab" Cakes

By now you have no doubt learned that fake crabmeat (those "crab sticks" found in most California sushi rolls) is not gluten-free. It also isn't the best option for creating a mock crab cake. This recipe makes a delicious cake that can be broiled or fried, a main dish or a perfect side. Treat it a lot like you would a stuffing recipe—get creative with your mix-ins and your spices to suit your taste, the flavors in your meal, and what's in your fridge!

3 cups zucchini, grated

½ cup mushrooms, chopped

⅓ cup onion, chopped

1 egg or egg substitute of choice (like Egg Substitute #7, page 16)

2 tablespoons sour cream (dairy or soy) or plain coconut yogurt

3 tablespoons mayonnaise or egg-free substitute

1 tablespoon chopped cilantro

2–3 tablespoons Old Bay seasoning, to taste

1 tablespoon lemon juice

1 cup gluten-free breadcrumbs (see page 78)

½ teaspoon sea salt

½ teaspoon black pepper

¼–½ cup Jules Gluten Free All Purpose Flour

3 tablespoons extra-virgin olive oil

▸ Grate the zucchini and press between paper towels to drain excess moisture.

▸ In a large bowl, combine the zucchini, mushrooms, onion, egg, sour cream, mayonnaise, cilantro, spices, and lemon juice. Stir in the breadcrumbs, adding slightly more or less until the mixture will hold together when squeezed into a patty. Form 8–10 patties and wrap individually in plastic wrap. Refrigerate or freeze until cold, at least 1 hour.

▸ Preheat the oven to 400°F. Pour the oil into a cast-iron skillet or other ovenproof metal pan and place in the oven to heat the oil. Scoop the flour into a flat-bottomed bowl and dredge each patty through the flour on both sides so that each patty is coated lightly with flour. Lay each dredged patty in the heated, oiled pan and place into the preheated oven. Bake for 10 minutes on one side, flip and bake another 5–10 minutes on the other side, until the patties are crispy and lightly browned. These may be fried over medium-high heat instead.

▸ Serve warm. Tartar sauce or spicy brown mustard are nice toppers, too!

SERVES 8–10

Curried Sweet Potato Pancakes

These add a great unexpected element to an otherwise everyday meal. Serve warm with applesauce for a cool finish.

2 large sweet potatoes, cleaned and grated

1 cup Jules Gluten Free All Purpose Flour (pages 6, 8)

2 teaspoons light brown sugar

1 teaspoon baking powder, gluten-free

¼ teaspoon turmeric

2 teaspoons curry powder

1 teaspoon ground cumin

1 teaspoon ground cinnamon

¼ teaspoon salt

Dash ground pepper

5 large eggs, beaten, or egg substitute of choice (like Egg Substitute #4, 5, or 7, pages 15–16)

¼ cup milk (dairy or nondairy)

1 teaspoon vanilla extract, gluten-free (only if using plain milk)

High heat canola oil for frying

Suggested Accompaniments:

Applesauce

Mango chutney or Mango Avocado Salsa (page 87)

Sour cream (dairy or nondairy)

▸ Wash and grate the sweet potatoes (skin on) in a food processor.

▸ In a large bowl, combine the gluten-free flour, sugar, baking powder, and spices. Add in the eggs, milk, and vanilla, if using, to the dry ingredients, then add the grated potatoes to the batter. If it is too thick, add more milk.

▸ Pour ⅛–¼ inch of oil into an electric skillet or deep skillet to cover the bottom. Heat the oil to 375–400°F over a medium-high flame. When hot, drop approximately 2 tablespoons of batter in circles and thin by spreading with the backside of a spoon. Cook each cake until lightly browned on each side, flipping to cook both sides evenly. Remove with a slotted spatula onto a paper towel–lined plate to cool.

▸ Serve warm with your accompaniment of choice.

SERVES 4

Eggplant Parmesan

You don't need to visit an expensive Italian restaurant to have memorable eggplant parmesan. This is the real deal.

EGGPLANT:

1 large eggplant (1½–1¾ pounds)

1 cup dry breadcrumbs, finely ground (see page 87)

½ cup Jules Gluten Free All Purpose Flour (pages 6, 8)

½ teaspoon salt

½ teaspoon freshly ground black pepper

2 large eggs or egg substitute of choice (like Egg Substitute #2 or 7, pages 15, 16)

2 tablespoons milk (dairy or nondairy)

High heat oil for frying

DISH:

1 jar pasta or marinara sauce, gluten-free (32 ounces) (or see Tomato Sauce recipe, page 167)

16 ounces fresh mozzarella cheese, sliced (dairy Buffalo or nondairy mozzarella flavor)

½ cup shredded or grated Parmesan cheese (dairy or nondairy)

Fresh basil leaves for layering in the dish

EGGPLANT:

▸ Wash eggplant and peel stripes in the skin, vertically, then cut lengthwise ¼–½ inch thick slices.

▸ Arrange one layer of cut eggplant slices in the bowl of a large colander; sprinkle evenly with salt.

▸ Repeat this process with the remaining slices, layering until all eggplant is in the colander. Place 2–3 heavy plates on top of the slices and set aside to help the eggplant release some moisture prior to cooking.

continues

DISH:

▸ Preheat the oven to 350°F.

▸ Remove each slice of eggplant and press between two paper towels to remove any remaining water and wipe off any excess salt. Prepare two wide, shallow bowls: one with breadcrumbs, flour, salt, and pepper; the other with egg and milk. Whisk each well.

▸ Heat a large skillet over medium heat and add ¼ inch of oil to preheat. When heated, dip both sides of the eggplant slices in the egg-milk bowl, then coat them both thoroughly in the flour-breadcrumb bowl.

▸ Gently lay each coated slice into hot oil and fry until golden brown, flipping to fry on both sides. Remove to drain on paper towels while finishing the remaining slices.

▸ Prepare a large 13 x 9-inch (or larger) baking dish by lightly spraying with cooking oil. Pour one-third of the marinara sauce, then layer one-third of the fried eggplant slices. Top eggplant with one-third of the mozzarella slices. Lay one basil leaf atop each circle of mozzarella then sprinkle with one-third of the Parmesan; repeat layers two more times.

▸ Bake uncovered for 30 minutes, or until hot and bubbly.

SERVES 6

Fish Sticks

This is a great recipe to get kids to eat more fish, or to make fish more portable, like for school lunches. It's a simple and quick recipe, too. Tartar Sauce or ketchup?

1 pound white fish fillets (like cod, tilapia, or orange roughy) cut into "fish-stick"-size strips (approximately 3 inches by 1 inch)

2 cups Jules Gluten Free All Purpose Flour (pages 6, 8)

1 tablespoon (or more) gluten-free seasoning (e.g., Konriko brand or Mrs. Dash, or just use salt and pepper)

2 large eggs or egg substitute of choice (like Egg Substitute #4 or 7, pages 15, 16), mixed

¼ cup milk (dairy or nondairy)

2 cups well-crushed gluten-free cereal (like Nature's Path Organic Corn Flakes Cereal, Corn or Rice Chex cereal, corn tortilla chips, or Food Should Taste Good Multi-Grain Chips)

High heat oil for frying

- ▶ Preheat the oven to 400°F (static) or 375°F (convection).

- ▶ Line a baking sheet with aluminum foil and spray with cooking oil. Rinse the fish, cut into strips, then pat dry. Set aside on a plate while mixing the rest of the toppings.

- ▶ Whisk gluten-free flour with the seasoning in a flat-bottomed bowl. Stir together the egg and milk in another bowl and place the crushed cornflakes in a third such bowl.

- ▶ Dredge the fish in the flour and seasoning bowl, then next in the eggs/milk bowl, and last in the crushed cornflakes bowl.

- ▶ In a large frying pan, heat the oil over a medium-high flame. Place each fish strip in the hot oil to flash fry on each side for crispness for 1–2 minutes, then place each stick onto a baking sheet lined with aluminum foil. Bake in the preheated oven for 10–15 minutes, or until the fish is flaky but not dry.

- ▶ Serve warm with ketchup, if desired.

SERVES 4

Fish Tacos

If you've had fish tacos in California, you're probably longing for some again. Make your own with your fish of choice, fillings of choice, and a great sauce! If you've not had a fish taco, you simply *must* try this recipe, and don't forget the cabbage. Trust me, it's exceptional and universally loved. This traditional batter recipe is a hit with kids, especially, but if you're looking for a bit healthier option, simply grill or broil your favorite fish, cut into bite-size pieces, squeeze lime on top, and combine with your favorite toppings to make a light and delicious option.

> 1 pound white fish (like tilapia or mahi mahi) cut into 1-inch pieces
> 1 lime
> 2 large eggs or egg substitute of choice (like Egg Substitute #4 or 7, pages 15, 16)
> ¼ cup Jules Gluten Free All Purpose Flour (pages 6, 8)
> ½ teaspoon salt
> High heat oil for frying
> 12 corn or gluten-free flour tortillas (page 126) or hard corn taco shells
> 2 tomatoes, chopped (preferably grape or cherry tomatoes)
> 1 avocado, chopped (or guacamole see page 85)
> Salsa
> Lettuce and/or cabbage, shredded
> ½ cup chopped fresh cilantro (optional)
> Sour cream (dairy or nondairy) (optional)

▶ Cut the fresh or thawed fish into pieces and place in a zip-top bag. Squeeze the lime into the bag with the fish, seal the bag, shake gently, and set aside to marinate.

▶ In a flat-bottomed bowl, stir the eggs and whisk in the gluten-free flour and salt.

▶ Prepare a large skillet or wok by heating the cooking oil over a medium-high flame. Dip the fish pieces into the egg batter and fry until cooked through and light brown, 3–5 minutes. Remove and drain on a paper plate or paper towels.

▶ Bake the hard taco shells according to package instructions, or wrap the soft tortillas in a towel and microwave for 20–30 seconds, until soft and warm. Add the fish and selected toppings and enjoy!

SERVES 4

Macaroni and Cheese

Ever a favorite of the younger set, this recipe can return to your table as a mild kid-friendly or a more mature adult version of typical macaroni and cheese. The beauty of making it fresh at home is that you can modify the taste to suit your audience and their dietary restrictions. There are some great gluten-free pastas on the market, and even several options for the traditional elbow noodle! As far as dairy-free cheeses go, these options are growing, too, with vegan cheeses hailing from Scotland (like Sheese brand cheeses in fourteen different flavor varieties), shakers of vegan Parmesan (some are even made from nuts!), and gluten-, dairy- and soy-free brands like Daiya that truly melt and taste great, too!

16 ounces gluten-free elbow pasta
(e.g., Ancient Harvest or Bionaturae)

2 tablespoons butter or nondairy alternative

¼ cup Jules Gluten Free All Purpose Flour (pages 6, 8)

2 cups milk (dairy or nondairy)

½ cup sour cream (dairy or nondairy) or plain coconut yogurt

1 teaspoon salt

½ teaspoon pepper

1½ cups cheddar cheese, shredded (or nondairy substitute)

½ cup mozzarella, Parmesan, fontina, or blend of other mild white cheeses (or nondairy substitute)

½ cup crushed gluten-free cereal (like Nature's Path Organic Corn Flakes Cereal Corn or Rice Chex cereal), corn tortilla chips, or Food Should Taste Good Multi-Grain Chips (optional as topping)

continues

▸ Preheat the oven to 375°F.

▸ Prepare the gluten-free pasta according to the package directions. Drain and set aside.

▸ Meanwhile, in a large saucepan, melt the butter over medium heat so as not to scald. Whisk in the flour and stir while cooking for 1–2 minutes. Add the milk and slowly bring to a gentle boil while stirring. Remove from the heat and stir in all the remaining ingredients. Add in the cooked pasta and pour into a 2-quart baking casserole.

▸ Bake in a preheated oven for 30 minutes. Crumble cereal or chips on top, if desired. Let stand to set and cool for 15 minutes before serving.

SERVES 6

Pad Thai

I view Pad Thai as the Thai version of "leftover night," only unlike typical leftover night, this is a dish everyone can get excited about. Open your refrigerator and start throwing ingredients into the wok or large skillet and sauté away.

There are many commercially available Pad Thai sauces found at Asian groceries and even mainstream supermarkets. Gluten- and dairy-free options from brands like Thai Kitchen are easy to find, just always double-check to see that there are no ingredient changes (like adding soy sauce, which often contains gluten) that would render it no longer gluten-free. Get creative, but be sure to write down what you do so you can repeat what is sure to be a new favorite dish!

Rice noodles (make as many as you like to complement this dish)

2 teaspoons toasted sesame oil

1 tablespoon extra-virgin olive oil

14 ounces cubed, unflavored tofu *or* 2 cups uncooked chicken *or* deveined shrimp

1½ cups mushrooms, chopped

1 teaspoon fresh ginger, peeled and chopped

8 ounces Pad Thai sauce (add more if the final dish is too dry)

1 tablespoon red chili paste

1 tablespoon granulated cane sugar

½ cup bok choy, spinach, kale, or other greens

1 cup mung or soy bean sprouts

Cilantro, chopped (optional)

Peanuts, chopped (optional; omit if making nut-free)

▸ Cook the rice noodles according to the package directions and set aside.

▸ Preheat a large wok or skillet and heat the sesame and olive oils over medium-high heat. Add tofu or chicken; if using shrimp, do not add it at this point. Sauté until lightly browned at the edges, then add the mushrooms or other chopped vegetables of your choice. Continue to sauté until tender, then add the ginger, sauce, chili paste, and sugar (add shrimp at this point, if using; cook for 3 minutes, until shrimp is pink).

▸ Just before serving, add the greens and bean sprouts, tossing with the other mixture until heated, approximately 1–2 minutes. Add cilantro and peanuts, if desired, as a garnish to each portion.

▸ Serve warm.

SERVES 4

Pot Pie

Pot pies were one of those rare comfort food treats I remember fondly from my childhood but have never had since going gluten-free. Why not make a new version I can enjoy with my family, no matter our dietary differences? This recipe is a universal favorite, eliciting such exclamations from teenagers as, "Is it Christmas or something?" and "My friend Tyler would marry you if he knew you were making pot pies!" The elementary schoolers even love these, and I love that I can clean out my refrigerator by putting just about anything in this stew. Add this recipe to your meal rotation and I promise everyone will be happy!

PASTRY (FOR TOP AND BOTTOM CRUSTS):

2¼ cups Jules Gluten Free All Purpose Flour (pages 6, 8)

1¼ teaspoons sea salt

⅔ cup shortening, butter, or nondairy alternative
   (often, a combination of shortening and butter or nondairy
   alternative produces a more flaky crust)

4–6 tablespoons water

PASTRY:

▸ In a large bowl, whisk together the gluten-free flour and salt. Cut in the butter with a pastry cutter until it makes a fine meal. Make a well in the center of the flour mixture and pour in the water, 1 tablespoon at a time. Using your fingers or a pastry cutter, squish the ingredients together until a smooth ball of dough is formed. Pull apart 10 smaller balls of dough and press into discs, wrap each tightly in plastic wrap, and set aside at room temperature for 30 minutes while preparing the stew.

continues

STEW:

1 cup diced potatoes

½–¾ cup onion, diced

½ cup celery, diced

1 cup sliced carrots

1 cup frozen green peas

1 cup sliced mushrooms

2 tablespoons extra-virgin olive oil

½ cup Jules Gluten Free All Purpose Flour

1 tablespoon cumin

1 teaspoon sea salt

½ teaspoon cracked black pepper

2 cups vegetable stock or chicken broth

¾ cup liquid creamer (dairy or nondairy) or half-and-half

½ cup gluten-free beer (e.g., Green's Ale) or ginger ale

4 cups combination of the following ingredients:

>   Chopped vegetables of choice
>
>   Boneless chicken breast halves, cubed
>
>   Sea scallops
>
>   Peeled shrimp, deveined and cut in thirds
>
>   Mussels or clams
>
>   Cleaned crabmeat
>
>   Fish fillets, cut into bite-size pieces

STEW:

▸ Prepare any previously frozen vegetables according to package directions. Cook potatoes and cut into bite-size chunks. Next, in a large saucepan, combine onions, celery, carrots, peas, mushrooms, potatoes, and any other vegetables; sauté in olive oil for 10 minutes, until the onions are translucent and the other vegetables are tender. Add flour to sautéed mixture, stirring well, then cook, stirring constantly, until thickened (if too thick, add more oil until mixture is able to be stirred easily with a spoon). Add broth and creamer, stirring into vegetable mixture. Remove from heat, and set aside.

▸ If using chicken, place in a pot and add water to cover; boil for 15 minutes. Remove from heat, drain, and add to vegetable mixture. If using mussels, boil separately for 2–3 minutes or 8–10 minutes for clams, or until they open. Once most are open, discard the ones that are still closed. Remove the mussels/clams from their shells and add to the vegetable mixture (note: often, the mussels/clams/scallops offer enough salt that no additional salt is

continues

necessary, but be sure to taste to see if any salt is needed before baking). Otherwise, in a saucepan over medium heat, add other seafood or combination totaling 4 cups into vegetable mixture. Cook over medium heat stirring constantly until thickened and bubbly.

▸ Preheat the oven to 350°F.

▸ Prepare five individual 4-inch ramekins. Press one small dough ball into the bottom and up the inside walls of each ramekin. This dough need not be pretty or consistent (or even pretty consistent); press into each ramekin to a thickness of approximately ⅛ inch. Prepare the filling as described, then fill the ramekins with the vegetable/chicken/or seafood mixture.

▸ Dust your clean counter or pastry mat and rolling pin liberally with gluten-free flour, then roll out the remaining balls of dough as top pastry crust circles to approximately ⅛–¼ inch thick. Gently lift and lay each circle of dough on top of filled ramekins and crimp the edges together with the bottom crust. Prick the top crust with a fork in three or four places to vent the steam. Brush the crust with milk (dairy or nondairy), egg white or olive oil.

▸ Bake the ramekins for 20–30 minutes, or until the top crust is lightly browned.

SERVES 5

Potato Gnocchi

This delicious comfort food is easier than you might think to prepare and is the perfect accompaniment for almost any sauce or main dish.

GNOCCHI:

1 pound Russet potatoes, sweet potatoes, or purple yams (2–3 medium-size), unpeeled and washed

1 cup Jules Gluten Free All Purpose Flour (pages 6, 8)

1 teaspoon sea salt

1 tablespoon extra-virgin olive oil

1 large egg or egg substitute of choice (like Egg Substitute # 1 or 7, pages 15, 16), beaten

----

Note: Sweet potatoes tend to need an extra 1½ cups flour; purple yams need extra ½ cup flour.

SAUCE:

2 tablespoons extra-virgin olive oil

10 ounces mushrooms, chopped

1¼ cups peas

2 cups cream (dairy or unflavored liquid nondairy creamer)

1 tablespoon fresh thyme, chopped

Sea salt and fresh ground pepper, to taste

1 tablespoon fresh chives, chopped

▸ To make the gnocchi, boil or microwave the washed potatoes (if microwaving, pierce potatoes with a fork in several places) until tender: approximately 20 minutes for boiling, 8 minutes for microwaving, depending on the power of your microwave. Set aside until cool enough to peel.

▸ Once cooled and peeled, place the potatoes in a large bowl and mash with a potato masher (or in a food processor) until there are no remaining lumps. Shake ¼ cup gluten-free flour over the top of the potatoes, along with the salt. Squish it together with your hands (or pulse it in a food processor) until incorporated with the potatoes. Continue adding flour by the ¼ cup full, incorporating until the full cup is added.

continues

▸ Form the potato mixture into a mound and make a well in the center. Pour the oil and beaten egg into the well and knead together until fully incorporated into the potato/flour mixture. It should no longer be wet but will hold together if you squeeze a handful together. If it is too wet, add more flour by the tablespoon; if it is too dry, add a touch of milk (dairy or nondairy).

▸ Flour a clean surface or pastry mat with gluten-free flour. Pat the potato mixture out to approximately ½-inch thickness and cut into strips approximately ½-inch wide. Cut each strip into ½-inch pieces. Take each piece and round the sides with the tines of a fork, to form tubular pieces like miniature barrels. Place each piece of formed gnocchi onto a parchment-lined baking sheet and when finished forming the pasta pieces, cover with a cloth and refrigerate until ready to boil.

▸ Bring a 6-quart pot of water to boil in preparation for the gnocchi. In a separate saucepan, heat the oil for the sauce over medium heat. Add the chopped mushrooms and sauté until lightly browned. Add the peas, cream, and thyme. Raise the temperature to medium-high and cook while stirring until the cream reduces by half. Season the sauce with salt and pepper, then remove from the heat.

▸ Meanwhile, place the gnocchi individually into the boiling water, boiling only enough pieces to cover the bottom of the pot so that it is not too crowded. The gnocchi are done when they float to the surface (approximately 5 minutes). Remove with a slotted spoon and serve warm with the sauce. Garnish with chives.

SERVES 4

Golden Potato Latkes (Potato Pancakes)

Latkes are just fancy hash browns (at least that's what I tell my kids!). They make a wonderful treat as a side or a main dish. Serve them with chunky applesauce, chutney, or Mango Avocado Salsa (see page 87) to accent other flavors in your meal.

2 cups grated gold or white potatoes (approximately 1½ pounds)

1 small onion, grated

3 eggs, beaten, or egg substitute of choice (like Egg Substitute #3, 4, or 5, page 15)

3 tablespoons Jules Gluten Free All Purpose Flour (pages 6, 8)

1 teaspoon sea salt

Pepper, to taste

1 teaspoon dried parsley flakes or 1½ teaspoons fresh parsley

⅛ cup grated Parmesan cheese or nondairy alternative (optional)

High heat cooking oil for frying

Applesauce or sour cream (dairy or nondairy) as a condiment

▸ Wash then grate the potatoes in a food processor, with the skins on or off—your choice. Grate the onion as well, then combine.

▸ Stir the beaten eggs with a fork, then combine in a large bowl with the potatoes and onion.

▸ In a separate bowl, whisk together the dry ingredients, including the parsley, and slowly stir into the potato mixture until combined. If the mixture is too dry to hold together, slowly add in small amounts of milk. The final mixture should hold together in a pancake shape when scooped into the hot oil.

▸ Pour about ⅛ inch of oil in an electric or deep skillet. Bring the oil to 375–400°F. Drop the potato mixture into the hot oil by large tablespoons, flattening the pancakes with the back of a spoon when in the oil. Cook each side until golden brown, flipping with a slotted spatula after 3–4 minutes per side.

▸ Remove the cooked latkes to a plate lined with paper towels. Keep warm in a warming drawer or low-temperature oven until ready to serve with applesauce or sour cream, if desired.

▸ The latkes may be frozen once cooked, blotted, and cooled. To reheat, cook on a baking sheet at 425°F (convection) or 450°F (static) for 15 minutes, turning repeatedly until crispy and hot.

MAKES APPROXIMATELY 15 LATKES

Crustless Quiche

This dish is one of my favorite go-to meals, as I can both empty my refrigerator and make a delicious and healthy meal in less than 45 minutes! Serve warm or cold, night or day! The optional nutritional yeast in this recipe is a great addition. Nutritional yeast has a creamy, cheese-like flavor and is an easy way to boost protein and B-vitamins in your foods.*

> 1 cup chopped vegetables of choice (broccoli, mushrooms, peppers, artichokes, squash, green beans, tomatoes, asparagus, etc.)
>
> 2 tablespoons onion, chopped
>
> 1 tablespoon extra-virgin olive oil
>
> Salt and pepper, to taste
>
> 1 teaspoon fresh or ½ teaspoon dried oregano
>
> 2 teaspoons fresh or 1 teaspoon dried basil
>
> 2 eggs or egg substitute of choice (like Egg Substitute #5, page 15)
>
> ½ cup sour cream (dairy or nondairy) or plain coconut yogurt
>
> 1 tablespoon Dijon mustard
>
> 1–2 tablespoons nutritional yeast
>   (optional, but recommended if not using dairy)
>
> ⅛ cup Jules Gluten Free All Purpose Flour (pages 6, 8)
>
> Plum tomatoes, sliced in thin circles for top of quiches
>
> Parmesan or nondairy alternative or nutritional yeast to sprinkle on top
>   (optional)

▸ Preheat the oven to 375°F (static) or 350°F (convection).

▸ Lightly butter or oil six 3- to 4-inch ramekins or one large pie or quiche pan (9–10 inches) and set aside.

continues

----

* Brewer's yeast is another option in recipes like this one, as it also adds nice flavor and contributes many valuable vitamins and minerals to any dish by adding as little as 2 tablespoons. Caution should be used when choosing a brewer's yeast, however, as most such products are actual by-products of beer brewing. Select brewer's yeasts such as Fearn's, which is grown on beet molasses instead, are gluten-free.

▸ Sauté the vegetables and onion in oil and season with salt, pepper, and herbs. Mix together the remaining ingredients (eggs, sour cream, mustard, nutritional yeast, and flour), then add in the sautéed vegetables.

▸ Spoon the vegetable/egg mixture into the pan or the ramekins, leaving ¼ inch from the top of the pan or cups. Lay one slice of tomato on the top of each mini-quiche, or in a circle on the top of the large quiche pan. Sprinkle lightly with Parmesan, if desired.

▸ Bake for approximately 45 minutes for the large quiche pan or 20 minutes for mini-quiches—until the crust edges are browning lightly and the quiche has puffed. Cool on a wire rack for at least 10 minutes before cutting and serving.

SERVES 6

See photo insert.

Easy Homemade Ravioli

Don't be afraid to make homemade pasta. Not only is this recipe quick and easy, it doesn't require any fancy ingredients and is practically allergen-free! This same recipe makes ravioli, tortellini, and even lasagne noodles!

1½ cups Jules Gluten Free All Purpose Flour (pages 6, 8)
1–2 tablespoons extra-virgin olive oil
½ cup very warm water
Salt for water
Filling of choice: pesto, hummus, tapenade, bruschetta, cheese and
    roasted peppers, etc.

▸ Pour gluten-free flour into a large bowl and form a shallow well in the flour. Add the oil and water a little at a time into the flour well and mix until it all comes together into a smooth ball. Wrap in clear plastic wrap and allow to rest for 30 minutes to 1 hour.

▸ Bring a large pot of water to boil with salt. Remove half of the pasta ball and leave the other half wrapped.

▸ For ravioli, prepare a clean counter or pastry mat by dusting with gluten free flour and roll into long, thin strips, (no thicker than ⅛ inch) cutting into equal-size squares. Drop a dollop of filling in the middle of every 2 squares, dab the edges with wet fingers, and press the two squares together to seal. Drop the sealed ravioli into boiling water.

▸ Cook for 2–4 minutes, until the ravioli float, then remove with a slotted spoon, drain and serve with your favorite sauce. Repeat with the other half of the dough.

▸ Note: These ravioli may be prepared ahead of time and refrigerated or frozen. Simply parboil them by boiling for only 2 minutes, drain, and allow to fully cool, then place sheets of wax paper between each ravioli and place in a freezer bag, seal and refrigerate or freeze. To serve, boil for 2 more minutes, or until they float.

SERVES 4

Shrimp Creole

Put on some Cajun music and make your family wonder what's gotten into you as you spread out all these yummy ingredients on your kitchen counter. Then treat them to something so good, so flavorful that they'll wonder how soon you'll do it all again.

4 tablespoons butter or nondairy alternative

2 tablespoons Jules Gluten Free All Purpose Flour (pages 6, 8)

½ teaspoon baking soda

⅓ cup chopped onion or ¼ cup dried onion

½ cup chopped celery or 1 teaspoon celery flakes

½ cup diced red, orange, or yellow pepper

½ cup corn kernels

2 cups chopped tomatoes or 1 (14-ounce) can chopped tomatoes

½ cup water

1 (4-ounce) can chopped green chiles (optional)

¾ teaspoon sea salt

Dash of pepper, to taste

1 teaspoon (or more) Creole seasoning, gluten-free (e.g., Konriko brand)

2 pounds uncooked shrimp, peeled and deveined, or white fish such as mahi mahi

2 cups cooked rice of your choice

▸ Melt 2 tablespoons butter in a large skillet over low heat. Add the gluten-free flour and baking soda, stirring until thickened and bubbly.

▸ In a separate pan, melt the remaining 2 tablespoons butter, then sauté the onion, celery, peppers, and corn and cook until tender. Combine those ingredients and the tomatoes, water, chiles (if using), and seasonings in a stockpot. Stir and cover to cook over medium heat for 5 minutes. Add the shrimp or fish and cook over medium heat until pink or cooked all the way through. Serve over rice.

SERVES 4

Stuffed Peppers with Quinoa

There aren't many ways to make peppers healthier, but stuffing them with nutrient-dense quinoa is one of them.

4–6 medium-large bell peppers (red, orange, yellow, or green, according to preference)
Extra-virgin olive oil
1 recipe Quinoa Salad (page 91 or page 92, either recipe)

▸ Preheat the oven to 325°F.

▸ Cut the caps off the peppers and remove the seeds from each pepper. Place the peppers cut side up in a steamer or on a steaming rack over an inch of water in a large, lidded pot. Cover, bring to a boil on the stovetop, then let steam for 10 minutes, just until soft, but not limp or mushy. Remove the peppers from the pan and set aside.

▸ Place each pepper into an oiled ovenproof baking dish. Fill each pepper with the quinoa salad mixture. Spoon any remaining quinoa salad around the peppers in the dish. Drizzle olive oil over the outsides of each pepper to help them brown during baking.

▸ Cover the baking dish with foil and bake for 20 minutes. Remove the foil and bake an additional 10 minutes.

▸ Serve warm.

SERVES 4–6

Sweet Potato and Black Bean Burritos

One way to get kids to eat healthier foods, like sweet potatoes and black beans, is to incorporate all that goodness in something universally appealing like burritos! I first tasted this combination at a restaurant in my college town. The memory of that amazing flavor combination has stayed with me for more years than I care to remember, making its way into many of my favorite dinner recipes, like this one.

2 large sweet potatoes
½ small onion, chopped
1 small red, orange, or yellow pepper, seeded and chopped
1 tablespoon extra-virgin olive oil
1 (15-ounce) can black beans, rinsed and drained
½ cup kernels of sweet corn, cooked
2 teaspoons Konriko Chipotle Seasoning (MSG-free) *or* 2 Sazón® Goya Coriander & Annatto Seasoning Packets (contains gluten-free MSG)
¾ cup chunky salsa
Gluten-free Flour Tortillas (see page 126)

▸ Parboil or microwave the sweet potatoes until they are fork tender, but not mushy. Allow them to cool and then peel and cut into small chunks.

▸ Sauté onion and peppers in olive oil until lightly browned. Add the sweet potatoes, beans, corn, and seasoning. Cook over medium heat until the potatoes are fully cooked and can be mashed. Mash them with a fork or leave as chunks of sweet potato. Add the salsa and heat until warm.

▸ Spoon into homemade Flour Tortillas or corn tortillas and serve warm as burritos, enchiladas, or quesadillas.

SERVES 4

Tempura Vegetables or Shrimp

Tempura is really beautiful food. Play with how much of the veggies you dip into the batter. This recipe is simple and, perhaps best of all, you get to drink the remaining beer with your meal!

> Broccoli florets, mushrooms, asparagus spears, or other vegetables of your choice or deveined raw shrimp
>
> ½ cup plus 2 tablespoons Jules Gluten Free All Purpose Flour (pages 6, 8)
>
> Salt and pepper, to taste
>
> 5 ounces Green's Quest Blonde Tripel Ale, Discovery Amber Ale, or other gluten-free beer of choice
>
> Extra-virgin olive oil for frying

▸ Cut the vegetables into 3-inch pieces or break the florets into bite-size portions. Wash the vegetables and set aside.

▸ In a shallow bowl, whisk the gluten-free flour with salt and pepper. Slowly pour in the beer and stir with a fork until it is thick enough to cling to your vegetables or shrimp without forming clumps of batter. If you find it is too thin, stir in more flour a teaspoon at a time; if too thick, add more beer, a teaspoon at a time.

▸ Pour enough olive oil into a wide sauté pan to cover your vegetables when placed in the hot oil. Heat oil over medium flame.

▸ Dip each vegetable or shrimp into the batter, coating the tops only of mushrooms or broccoli, and the entire stem of other vegetables. Gently submerge each battered piece in the hot oil and fry until the batter is light golden brown, turning once if necessary to fry the entire piece. This process should only take 1–2 minutes for each piece; slightly longer for shrimp, which should cook until pink throughout.

▸ Remove the hot vegetables or shrimp from the oil when done and lay on a plate covered with a paper towel to absorb excess oil. Place the drained pieces onto a baking sheet and keep them warm in a warming drawer or oven on low until ready to serve.

▸ Refrigerate any uneaten pieces and reheat for another day.

SERVES 4–6

See photo insert.

Thai Vegetable Curry

I often count on curry to lend its distinctive flavor to all kinds of recipes. The tofu adds important protein, and the veggies give welcome vitamins and minerals. And did I mention how good this dish is as leftovers? The curry becomes even more aromatic, making this one of those rare recipes that tastes even better the next day!

2–3 tablespoons extra-virgin olive oil

14 ounces firm, drained tofu, cut into cubes, *or* 2 cups cubed chicken or deveined shrimp (optional)

1 red, orange, or yellow pepper, cut into strips

1 cup chopped bok choy stems and leaves
   (separate the stems and leaves for sautéing)

1–2 large portobello mushroom caps, chopped

1 cup corn, peas, or edamame (soy beans)

1 tablespoon granulated cane sugar

1–2 tablespoons red curry paste, gluten-free (to taste)

7 ounces coconut milk

Rice or rice noodles

2 tablespoons chopped fresh basil leaves

2 tablespoons salted chopped peanuts (optional; omit if making nut-free)

▸ Heat 2 tablespoons of oil in a large skillet or wok over medium-high heat. Add the tofu or chicken (if using) and cook until beginning to brown slightly. Prepare the vegetables and portobello mushroom caps, adding to the hot oil the bell pepper strips, bok choy stems, and portobello.

▸ Sauté until the bok choy stems are softening and the peppers are browning a bit (if using chicken, cook until it is no longer pink inside). If necessary, add the remaining oil to the pan and heat. Add the shrimp (if using), corn, bok choy leaves, sugar, and red curry paste. Sauté for another 2–3 minutes, stirring periodically so that nothing burns and shrimp is pink.

▸ Pour in the coconut milk. Combine well and serve over rice or prepared Asian rice noodles when the milk has heated and the mixture is thickened (approximately 5 minutes). Sprinkle the basil and peanuts (if using) on top of the dish just before serving.

SERVES 4

Tomato Sauce

Serve this sauce with your favorite pasta, chicken, pizza (see dough, page 116) or Eggplant Parmesan (page 146), or simply use as a dipping sauce for Fish Sticks (page 148).

> ½ medium onion, peeled and diced
>
> 2 tablespoons extra-virgin olive oil
>
> 4 cups diced fresh tomatoes (or two 14.5-ounce cans whole peeled and drained or diced tomatoes)
>
> 12 ounces (1 can) tomato paste
>
> 3 sprigs fresh leaf basil, chopped (or 1 teaspoon dried leaf basil)
>
> 1 teaspoon dried leaf oregano, crumbled
>
> Minced garlic, to taste
>
> Salt and pepper, to taste

▸ Prepare the tomato sauce by sautéing the diced onion with olive oil until tender, then dicing the tomatoes and adding them to the pot with the remaining ingredients and salt and pepper to taste. Cook uncovered on medium-low heat for at least 15 minutes, or until ready to serve in a dish. Cook longer if the sauce is too thin.

SERVES 4

6

Desserts

Angel Food Cake with a Twist

Liqueurs and liquor (distilled*) are excellent ways of introducing subtle flavors in unexpected places! And with the orange rind and chocolate in this fantastic recipe, you'll probably find yourself inventing cake-making occasions to try out all the possible twists!

1¼ cups Jules Gluten Free All Purpose Flour (pages 6, 8)
2 tablespoons cocoa powder (omit if using bourbon)
2 tablespoons orange rind
½ cup confectioners' sugar
6 large eggs, separated
1 cup granulated cane sugar
¼ cup boiling water
3 tablespoons gluten-free Irish Cream Liqueur, Kahlúa, or bourbon

▸ Preheat the oven to 300°F (convection, preferred) or 325°F (static).

▸ Sift gluten-free flour, cocoa (if using), orange rind, and confectioners' sugar together in a small bowl and set aside.

▸ Separate the eggs, beating the whites in a stainless steel bowl using a clean whisk attachment to an electric mixer until stiff peaks form (approximately 6–8 minutes, depending on the mixer speed), then set that bowl aside. In a separate bowl, beat the yolks and the granulated sugar until light. Next, add the boiling water and liqueur to the yolk mixture, beating until blended. Finally, stir in the flour mixture until incorporated.

continues

----

* Distilled alcohols are rendered gluten-free. Consult with each product manufacturer's website to determine whether or not additional gluten-containing ingredients have been added to the liqueur/liquor after distillation, which would make the product no longer gluten-free.

▸ Fold the beaten whites into the mixture by gently stirring with a rubber spatula. When mixed, pour into an ungreased 10-inch tube or springform pan. Bake for 30 minutes, then increase the heat to 325°F (convection, preferred) or 350°F (static) and bake for another 20–25 minutes, or until a cake tester comes out clean.

▸ Invert the pan and allow to cool before removing the cake by gently sliding a knife around the outside of the cake to release the cake from the sides. Use Cream Cheese Glaze or serve plain, with berries or in a Trifle (see page 234).

SERVES 8–10

Cream Cheese Glaze (optional):

8 ounces cream cheese (dairy or nondairy)
1 cup confectioners' sugar
½ cup heavy cream (dairy or nondairy, like MimicCreme—vegan, dairy-, and soy-free but contains nuts)
Chocolate shavings (optional)

▸ Whip the cream cheese and sugar until smooth then slowly stir in only enough cream to make a spreadable consistency. Drizzle over the cake and sprinkle chocolate shavings on top.

Apple Cranberry Cobbler

I've used apples and cranberries in this recipe, but feel free to substitute with other berries and pears, for example, to make an equally delicious dessert.

FRUIT FILLING:

2 cups fresh cranberries

⅛ cup granulated sugar

4 apples, peeled and chopped into large chunks
   (firm apples like Fuji, Gala, or Jonagold)

½ cup brown sugar

2 tablespoons Jules Gluten Free All Purpose Flour (pages 6, 8)

⅓ cup fresh orange juice

COBBLER:

1 cup Jules Gluten Free All Purpose Flour (pages 6, 8)

1 cup granulated sugar

Cinnamon, to taste

1 large egg or egg substitute of choice (like Egg Substitute #1, 2, or 4,
   page 15), beaten

¼ cup butter or nondairy alternative, melted

▸ Preheat the oven to 350°F (static) or 325°F (convection).

▸ Place the cranberries in a small pot on your stove over medium heat. Add the sugar, stir and cover, cooking and stirring occasionally until the berries begin to pop and the mixture thickens a bit. Remove from the heat and add to a large bowl with the chopped apples. Add the brown sugar, 2 tablespoons gluten-free flour, and orange juice. Stir, then pour into an oiled 8 x 8-inch baking dish.

▸ In a separate bowl, whisk together gluten-free flour, sugar, and cinnamon. Add the egg and stir with a fork until the mixture is crumbly. Crumble over the fruit, then drizzle the melted butter over the top.

▸ Bake until the cobbler is lightly browned and the fruit is bubbly, 30–45 minutes. Serve warm with or without ice cream.

SERVES 6

Apple or Berry Pie

If you have a farmers' market in your area, or can pick your own fruit, there is nothing much better than making a fresh fruit pie. Use My Grandma's Pie Crust recipe in this book (see page 222) and double it for fruit pies like apple, which are well suited to a top crust. Roll the top pastry out for a solid crust, or choose a lattice design—either way, if there are cracks in the crust, simply cut out leftover pastry with small decorative cookie cutters, dab the pastry with water, and lay on top of the cracks to disguise them deliciously!

As far as apples go, select the freshest and firmest apples available according to the time of year. Some good choices include Granny Smith, Golden Delicious, Rome, Braeburn, Jonagold, Gala, and Fuji. Berry pies are delicious when mixed with different available berries, but as with anything else, use the freshest berries available for the best outcome.

PIE FILLING:

5 large or 7–8 small tart apples, peeled, cored,
    and sliced (approximately 2–3 pounds) or 1–1½ quarts fresh berries,
    washed and drained
1 cup granulated cane sugar
1½ tablespoons cinnamon
¼ teaspoon salt
½ cup Jules Gluten Free All Purpose Flour (pages 6, 8)
1 tablespoon apple cider vinegar or lemon juice
2 recipes of My Grandma's Pie Crust (page 222)

▸ Peel, core, and slice the apples. While you are slicing the apples, put the cut apples in a bowl filled with cold water and 1 tablespoon of lemon juice to keep them from turning brown while you are slicing the rest of the apples.

▸ Drain the apples, or alternatively, wash and drain the berries; toss the fruit with the remaining ingredients. Set aside to help juices to form while finishing the crust.

continues

▸ Roll out half of the pastry dough and line a pie plate, leaving some overhang. Fill the pastry-lined pie pan with prepared fruit mixture (for apples, mound them higher in the center of the pie plate). Roll out the top crust, then place as a solid crust or in a lattice design carefully over the filling and flute the edges or press with the tines of a fork to decoratively seal together the top and bottom crusts. Cut 3 or 4 slits in the top. Brush the top with milk of choice or mixed egg wash (1 egg mixed with 2 tablespoons water).

▸ Bake in a preheated 450° oven for 10 minutes. Reduce the heat to 350° and bake 25 minutes longer for berry pie; 35 to 45 minutes longer for apple pie. Cover the edges of the crust with aluminum foil or a pie crust saver until there are only 10 minutes left of baking. Brush the crust with milk or egg wash every 15 minutes during baking to help it to brown nicely. Remove to cool on a wire rack and sprinkle lightly with demerera or granulated cane sugar, if desired.

SERVES 6–8

See photo insert.

Berry Coulis

These simple ingredients work magic together in a coulis that will add that special touch atop Key Lime Pie (see page 214), Apple or Berry Pie (see page 273), Cheesecake (see page 191), ice cream, or even just yogurt.

¾ cup fresh berries of choice
⅓ cup granulated cane sugar
1 teaspoon vanilla extract, gluten-free

▸ Combine all the ingredients in a small heavy saucepan and stir over medium heat until the sugar crystals have dissolved. Simmer while stirring for an additional 3–4 minutes.

▸ Transfer to a covered bowl and refrigerate until serving.

SERVES 4

Chocolate Birthday Cake

Happy birthday to someone, happy birthday to someone, happy birthday dear someone, happy birthday to you! Birthday cake is not just reserved for that special someone's special day—make this light chocolate cake anytime the urge hits you! To bake an egg-free birthday cake, try my Eggless Cake recipe, page 204.

3 cups Jules Gluten Free All Purpose Flour (pages 6, 8)
¼ cup powdered milk (dairy or nondairy)
1 tablespoon baking powder, gluten-free
¼ cup cocoa powder
¼ teaspoon salt
½ cup butter or nondairy alternative
2 cups granulated cane sugar
4 large eggs
2 teaspoons vanilla extract, gluten-free
1¼ cups chocolate milk (dairy or nondairy)

▸ Preheat the oven to 350°F (static) or 325°F (convection). Spray two 7- or 9-inch round cake pans with nonstick cooking spray and dust the entire surface of any non-silicone pans lightly with gluten-free flour to help remove the cake after baking. For a higher crown on each cake, use the smaller 7-inch pans.

▸ Whisk together the flour, powdered milk, baking powder, cocoa, and salt and set aside.

▸ In a large mixing bowl, combine the butter and sugar and beat well with the paddle attachment on an electric mixer, until the mixture is very light and fluffy (approximately 3–4 minutes). Add the eggs next, one at a time, beating well after each addition. Mix in the vanilla with the last egg addition. Slowly add the milk, alternating with the flour mixture, and beating in between the additions. Beat on high speed until smooth and pour into the prepared pans.

▸ Bake for 30 minutes, turning the pans halfway through if using a convection setting. To test the cakes for doneness, insert a cake tester or toothpick into the middle of each cake and be sure it comes out clean, with no wet crumbs attached. The cakes will also begin to pull away slightly from the sides of the pans when done. Add time if necessary to fully bake the cakes.

continues

▶ When done, turn off the oven and leave the oven door open to let the cakes cool slowly for 10 minutes or so, then remove the cake pans to a cooling rack. After 20–30 minutes of total cooling time, gently invert the cakes in their pans to remove them from the pans, then flip gently back onto the cooling rack until fully cooled. Frost the cakes only when fully cooled, or in the alternative, wrap the cooled cakes with wax paper or plastic wrap, then seal inside freezer bags to freeze or refrigerate until ready to use.

SERVES 10

See photo insert.

White Frosting

While there are some brands of ready-made gluten-free frostings available, there is no reason to spend the extra money when real, old-fashioned frosting is this easy and cheap to make. There is no substitute for the real thing!

½ cup butter or nondairy alternative, softened
2½ cups confectioners' sugar
1½ teaspoons vanilla extract, gluten-free
Up to ¼ cup milk (dairy or nondairy)
Food coloring (optional)

▶ Cream the butter and sugar together with an electric mixer. Add the vanilla and 2 tablespoons of milk, beating well to combine, then add food coloring (if desired) and more milk (if and as necessary) to achieve a spreadable consistency, beating for several minutes at the end until it is light and fluffy.

MAKES 3 CUPS FROSTING

continues

Chocolate Frosting

▶ Use White Frosting base and add ½ cup cocoa powder. Follow white frosting directions.

MAKES 3 CUPS FROSTING

Mocha Frosting

▶ Use White Frosting base, but substitute cold coffee, cappuccino, or espresso for the milk. Add ¼ cup cocoa to the base as well.

MAKES 3 CUPS FROSTING

White Birthday Cake

Hands-down, one of my favorite recipes! I find any reason to celebrate if it means I can make this cake. It is easily made into a double layer cake, a sheet cake, or any kind of decorative cake pan (I have personally made castles, bows, a pirate ship, a Pokémon ball, Spider-Man, and downtown buildings out of this recipe!). To bake an egg-free birthday cake, try my Eggless Cake recipe, page 204.

CAKE:

3 cups Jules Gluten-Free All Purpose Flour (pages 6, 8)

¼ cup powdered milk (dairy or nondairy)

1 tablespoon baking powder, gluten-free

¼ teaspoon salt

½ cup butter or nondairy alternative

2 cups granulated cane sugar

4 large eggs

2 teaspoons vanilla extract, gluten-free

1 cup milk (dairy or nondairy)

▸ Preheat the oven to 350°F (static) or 325°F (convection). Spray two 7- or 9-inch round cake pans with nonstick cooking spray and dust the entire surface of any non-silicone pans lightly with gluten-free flour to help remove the cake after baking. For a higher crown on each cake, use the smaller 7-inch pans.

▸ Whisk together the flour, powdered milk, baking powder, and salt and set aside.

▸ In a large mixing bowl, combine the butter and sugar and beat well with the paddle attachment, until the mixture is very light and fluffy (approximately 3–4 minutes). Add the eggs next, one at a time, beating well after each addition. Mix in the vanilla with the last egg addition. Slowly add the milk, alternating with the flour mixture and beating in between the additions. Beat on high speed until smooth and pour into the prepared pans.

▸ Bake for 30 minutes, turning the pans halfway through if using a convection setting. To test the cakes for doneness, insert a cake tester or toothpick in the middle of each cake and be sure it comes out clean, with no wet crumbs attached. The cakes will also begin to pull away slightly from the sides of the pans when done. Add time if necessary to fully bake the cakes.

continues

▸ When done, turn off the oven and leave the oven door open to let the cakes cool slowly for 10 minutes or so, then remove the cake pans to a cooling rack. After 20–30 minutes of total cooling time, gently invert the cakes in their pans to remove them from the pans, then flip gently back onto the cooling rack until fully cooled. Frost the cakes only when fully cooled, or in the alternative, wrap the cooled cakes with wax paper or plastic wrap, then seal inside freezer bags to freeze or refrigerate until ready to use.

SERVES 10

(For frosting options, see pages 177–178).

Blueberry Buckle

The Blueberry Buckle is an old-timey favorite in the coffee cake family—a single-layer cake with a streusel-type topping. As the cake bakes, some of the topping sinks to the bottom of the pan, which makes the streusel "buckle" on top. A great way to celebrate healthy, delicious blueberries when in season, or use frozen blueberries and pretend it's warm outside!

CAKE:

4 cups fresh blueberries

4 cups plus 2 tablespoons of Jules Gluten Free All Purpose Flour (pages 6, 8)

2 tablespoons baking powder, gluten-free

1 teaspoon salt

½ cup unsalted butter or nondairy alternative, softened

1½ cups granulated cane sugar

2 large eggs or egg substitute of choice (like Ener-G Egg Replacer and/or Egg Substitute #1 or 2, page 15)

1¼ cups milk (dairy or nondairy)

TOPPING:

½ cup unsalted butter or nondairy alternative, softened

1 cup granulated cane sugar

⅔ cup Jules Gluten Free All Purpose Flour (pages 6, 8)

1 teaspoon cinnamon

▸ Preheat the oven to 375°F (static) or 350°F (convection).

▸ Oil a 9-inch springform pan and have a small, oiled 6-inch square baking pan or casserole ready, in the event you have too much batter for just one pan.

▸ Toss the berries with 2 tablespoons of gluten-free flour and set aside.

continues

▸ Combine the 4 cups of gluten-free flour, baking powder, and salt and set aside.

▸ Cream the butter and sugar until fluffy, approximately 3 minutes.

▸ Beat in the eggs, and once incorporated, add the flour mixture, alternating with milk. Fold in the floured berries last (stir gently, to prevent the blueberry color from coloring the batter).

▸ Pour the batter into the prepared pan(s). Set aside.

▸ Combine the topping ingredients with a fork to make a crumbly mixture. Sprinkle evenly over the batter.

▸ Bake a small pan for approximately 40 minutes and a 9-inch springform for 50 minutes, or until a cake tester inserted into the center of each pan comes out clean (some of the streusel may still stick to the tester).

SERVES 6–8

Best Brownies Ever

No matter how you like your brownies—cake-like or fudgy—these brownies will please you. They have an amazing, slightly crispy top and chewy, deliciously decadent and moist centers. I'm craving chocolate just thinking about them! What a fantastic treat to take to your next party or picnic, but you may want to double the recipe so there are some left for you!

2 ounces unsweetened chocolate
(for nondairy, use two 100 percent cacao baking squares)

½ cup chocolate chips (dairy or nondairy, e.g., Sunspire or Enjoy Life)

8 tablespoons unsalted butter or nondairy alternative

1 cup granulated cane sugar

2 teaspoons vanilla extract, gluten-free

2 large eggs or egg substitute of choice (like Ener-G Egg Replacer and/or Egg Substitute #1, 2, 3, 4, or 5, page 15)

¼ cup black coffee, prepared

⅔ cup Jules Gluten Free All Purpose Flour (pages 6, 8)

½ teaspoon salt

1 teaspoon baking powder, gluten-free

¾ cup walnuts, pecans, or macadamia nuts
(optional; omit if making nut-free)

▸ Preheat the oven to 325°F (static).

▸ Arrange a sheet of parchment paper or aluminum foil in an 8 x 8-inch baking pan, pressing to cover the bottom and up the sides. If using aluminum foil, use the "release" kind, or lightly spray with cooking oil. This step will make it easier to remove the brownies from the pan by pulling up on the paper or foil and leaving behind a clean pan.

▸ Prepare a double boiler or a medium-size pan filled with 1 inch of water, with a slightly smaller pan sitting on top of the pan with water. Boil the water in the bottom pan, then cut the flame back to low-medium and add the chocolates and butter to the top pan over the simmering water. Stir and remove from heat when melted.

continues

▸ In a separate bowl, whisk together the sugar and vanilla, then stir in the eggs, one at a time. Finally, add in the coffee and continue to whisk until the mixture is completely smooth.

▸ In a large bowl, whisk to combine the flour, salt, and baking powder. Stir in the melted chocolate mixture and the sugar mixture until combined. Gently stir in the nuts, if using.

▸ Pour the batter into the prepared pan and bake for 35–45 minutes, or until a toothpick or cake tester inserted in the center comes out with only a few wet crumbs (not totally clean, or they'll be overcooked!).

▸ As a rule, brownies are much better on the un-done side, as opposed to the overdone side.

▸ Cool brownies in the pan on a wire rack for 5 minutes. Lift the brownies from the pan by pulling up on the paper or foil. Completely cool brownies on a wire rack. Cut into squares with a clean knife and serve.

MAKES APPROXIMATELY 16–20 BROWNIES

Buckeyes

These traditionally peanut butter—based candies are loved by all, but have been previously off-limits to the food allergic. Follow these simple modifications to make this wonderful treat enjoyable to all at your holiday table!

If you are avoiding nuts, sunflower "nut" butter and soy "nut" butter are tasty alternatives to peanut butter, but their consistencies are somewhat thinner, so the freezing steps in this recipe are essential to making pretty, not sticky, balls. Leave yourself some extra time to ensure you have time to freeze the balls in between each step, as noted.

> 1 (16-ounce) jar creamy sunflower "nut" butter, soy "nut" butter, or use peanut butter if not making nut-free
> 8 tablespoons (½ cup) shortening
> 1 pound (1 box) confectioners' sugar
> ¼ cup Jules Gluten Free All Purpose Flour (pages 6, 8)
> 1 tablespoon vanilla extract, gluten-free
> 10 ounces chocolate chips (dairy or nondairy, e.g., Sunspire or Enjoy Life)
> 1 tablespoon canola oil

▸ Cream the nut butter and the shortening. If your shortening is refrigerated, bring it to room temperature before creaming. Beat together with the sugar, flour, and vanilla; mix until light and fluffy (approximately 3–5 minutes).

▸ Divide into four equal amounts and wrap each tightly in plastic wrap. Refrigerate or freeze until very cold.

▸ Prepare a cookie sheet by lining it with wax paper.

▸ Removing only one of the four portions, pinch off a tablespoon at a time of the nut butter mixture and roll gently in your hands to form a ball. Place on the prepared cookie sheet. When all the balls have been formed, repeat with the other portions from the refrigerator or freezer to fill the sheet. When the sheet is filled, cover with plastic wrap and then aluminum foil and place in the freezer until the balls are very cold or soft-frozen. Repeat if necessary with additional pans to finish the nut butter mixture.

continues

▸ Using a double-boiler or placing a small saucepan in a slightly larger saucepan one-third filled with water, heat the water over low-medium heat. Melt the chocolate slowly in the smaller saucepan over the heated water. Stir in the canola oil when the chocolate has melted. Stir periodically to keep it evenly mixed and liquefied.

▸ When the balls are soft-frozen, remove one tray from the freezer and pick up one ball at a time by inserting a toothpick into the middle of the ball. Gently swirl the ball through the melted chocolate, covering the ball, but leaving the top center (about one-third of the ball) uncovered by chocolate. Replace onto the wax paper–lined cookie sheet. Repeat with all the balls. When they are all dipped, recover with the plastic wrap and foil and replace in the freezer.

▸ Serve cold, but not frozen. If these balls become warmer than room temperature, they will begin to sweat, so be sure to serve with toothpicks!

MAKES APPROXIMATELY 2 DOZEN BUCKEYES

See photo insert.

Candy Cupcakes

This is the perfect post-Halloween candy recycling recipe! There are many companies now making gluten- and dairy-free confections, but if you find it difficult to get your hands on chocolate candies that meet your particular dietary restrictions, just use my Buckeyes recipe (see page 185) and cut the prepared buckeyes into smaller pieces, creating gluten-free, dairy-free, nut-free, egg-free "nut" butter cup pieces just perfect for this recipe! Another easy solution for you chocoholics: chop a chocolate bar into pieces however large you like (Enjoy Life even has a dairy-, gluten-, soy-, and nut-free chocolate bar, so there are plenty of options).

2 tablespoons unsweetened cocoa powder

½ cup milk (dairy or nondairy)

4 large eggs or egg substitute of choice

½ cup canola oil

2 teaspoons vanilla extract, gluten-free

1 cup granulated cane sugar

2⅔ cups Jules Gluten Free All Purpose Flour (pages 6, 8)

1 tablespoon baking powder, gluten-free

Dash of salt

1 package (3.4 ounces) vanilla instant pudding, gluten-free (some brands like Jell-O are currently dairy-free as well)

1 cup Reese's Peanut Butter Cups or other chocolate candy of choice, chopped

▶ Preheat the oven to 325°F.

▶ In a large mixing bowl stir the cocoa powder in with the milk, then add eggs, oil, and vanilla together until all the liquid ingredients are well blended. Whisk together the other dry ingredients in a separate bowl, then slowly pour into the liquid bowl and mix using the medium speed of an electric mixer for 2 minutes, until very thick. Gently fold in the chopped candy.

continues

- Oil or line with cupcake papers two muffin tins (twenty-four muffin cups) and fill with the cupcake batter one-half to two-thirds full.

- Bake in a preheated oven for approximately 20 minutes. The tops should be lightly browned and they should have crowned. Stick a toothpick or cake tester to the bottom of the muffin cups to be sure they are done; there should be very little crumb attached to the toothpick.

- Remove to cool on a wire rack and frost with Nut Butter Frosting or White or Chocolate Frosting (see pages 177–178) when fully cooled.

MAKES 24 CUPCAKES

Nut Butter Frosting

½ cup creamy peanut butter, soy "nut" butter, or sunflower "nut" butter
½ cup butter or nondairy alternative, room temperature
2 cups confectioners' sugar
1 teaspoon vanilla extract, gluten-free
3 tablespoons milk (dairy or nondairy)
Colorful candies to sprinkle on top

- Mix together all the ingredients except milk and candies until smooth. Gradually add milk, 1 tablespoon at a time, until of a spreadable consistency. Depending on what kind of nut butter you use you may need to add more or less milk.

- Frost the cupcakes and sprinkle with other colorful candies . . . enjoy!

MAKES APPROXIMATELY 2 CUPS FROSTING

Carrot–Apple Cider Cake

Full of carrots, apples, and other fresh textures, this cake is moist, full of Fall flavor, and oh-so-versatile. Try this cake in a bundt pan or a sheet pan, frost it or not—it's delicious any way you slice it. Enjoy!

¾ cup sweet (not tart) peeled and chopped apples (like Gala, Fuji, Jonathan, or Honeycrisp)

1¼ cups peeled and chopped carrots

½ cup raisins or dried cranberries

½ cup unsweetened coconut, grated

8 tablespoons butter or nondairy alternative

⅔ cup granulated cane sugar

3 large eggs or egg substitute of choice (like Ener-G Egg Replacer and/or Egg Substitute #1 or 2, page 15)

⅔ cup apple cider, carbonated and gluten-free (e.g., Samuel Smith's Organic Apple Cider)

2½ cups Jules Gluten Free All Purpose Flour (pages 6, 8)

½ teaspoon baking soda

2 teaspoons baking powder, gluten-free

2 teaspoons cinnamon

1 teaspoon pumpkin pie spice

▸ Preheat the oven to 350°F (static) or 325°F (convection).

▸ Oil a 9 x 13-inch baking pan or bundt pan.

▸ In a large food processor, chop the apples and carrots. Mix together in a bowl with the raisins and coconut and set aside.

▸ Cream the butter and the sugar until light and fluffy. Mix in the eggs and blend until incorporated. Stir in the carrot-raisin mixture. Pour in the apple cider and mix. Gradually stir in the gluten-free flour together with the remaining dry ingredients.

▸ Pour the batter into the prepared pan and use a rubber spatula to smooth the top. Bake in the preheated oven for 20–30 minutes, just until a cake tester inserted into the center of the cake comes out clean.

▸ When cooled, frost with Sour Cream Frosting.

SERVES 10

continues

Sour Cream Frosting

3 cups confectioners' sugar

4 tablespoons butter or nondairy alternative

½ cup sour cream (dairy or nondairy) or coconut yogurt

2 teaspoons vanilla extract, gluten-free

½ teaspoon lemon juice (optional)

¼ teaspoon salt

½ teaspoon grated lemon zest (optional)

¼ teaspoon cream of tartar (if using nondairy sour cream or coconut yogurt)

▸ In a medium bowl, sift the confectioners' sugar. With an electric mixer, beat the other ingredients, to incorporate, then slowly stir in the confectioners' sugar, beating until smooth. Add more confectioners' sugar if the frosting is too thin.

MAKES 3 CUPS FROSTING

Cheesecake—Dairy-Free
and Delicious!

Those who may enjoy traditional dairy-full cheesecakes may not be able to appreciate the void left in the lives of those who cannot partake of this cow's milk creamy delicious dessert, so often the conduit for heavenly sauces, berries, and other sinful sweets like chocolate! For those in the latter camp, here's a safe and delicious soy alternative just begging to be smothered by your favorite accompaniments!

While I use granola here as the crust, feel free to use a traditional Graham Cracker Pie Crust (see page 214).

GRANOLA CRUST:

1½ cups gluten-free Granola (see recipe, page 53)
1½ tablespoons dairy-free butter alternative, melted

CHEESECAKE:

16 ounces (2 cups) firm silken tofu
8 ounces (1 cup) soy cream cheese (plain)
4 ounces (½ cup) soy sour cream (plain)
2 tablespoons Jules Gluten Free All Purpose Flour (pages 6, 8)
⅔ cup confectioners' sugar
½ cup granulated cane sugar
2 teaspoons vanilla extract, gluten free
½ teaspoon lemon, lime, or orange peel (optional)
¾ cup dairy-free chocolate chips (e.g., Sunspire or Enjoy Life) (optional)
2 cups fresh berries for topping or 1 recipe Berry Coulis (page 175)

continues

- To make the crust, grind the gluten-free granola into a small fine-size by pulsing in a blender or food processor. Add the melted butter alternative and pulse until sticky. Press into the bottom of a 9-inch pan and set aside.

- To make the cheesecake, bring all the ingredients to room temperature.

- Preheat the oven to 325°F (static).

- Blend the tofu, cream cheese, sour cream, and gluten-free flour together until smooth, either in a food processor or a stand mixer. Add the sugars and vanilla and blend well. Stir in the citrus peel and chocolate chips last, if using.

- Pour into the prepared crust—fill only two-thirds of the pie pan; if there is extra filling, oil a small ramekin and pour the remaining filling into the ramekin to bake. Bake for 50 minutes, or until lightly browned and only slightly jiggly in the center. Turn the oven off, but leave the cheesecake in the oven for 1 more hour. Then remove to fully cool to room temperature before refrigerating. Top with berries or berry coulis just before serving.

Chocolate and Raspberry Tart

I like using a touch of mesquite flour in tart dough, as it helps it to brown nicely. Mesquite flour also adds a slightly chocolate note to the tart and some nutritional benefits as well. If you can't get your hands on any of this flour, though, simply substitute another gluten-free flour such as buckwheat or my all-purpose blend.

TART CRUST:

2 tablespoons mesquite flour (or use buckwheat flour or
   Jules Gluten Free All Purpose Flour, pages 6, 8)

⅞ cup Jules Gluten Free All Purpose Flour

2 tablespoons unsweetened cocoa powder

3 tablespoons granulated cane sugar

¼ teaspoon salt

½ cup unsalted butter or nondairy alternative

1 egg yolk or egg yolk substitute of choice
   (like Egg Substitute #10, 11, or 12, page 17)

1 tablespoon ice water

TART FILLING:

12 ounces bittersweet chocolate, coarsely chopped (dairy or nondairy)

1½ cups heavy whipping cream (dairy or nondairy alternative like
   MimicCreme—vegan, dairy-, and soy-free but contains nuts)

2 tablespoons unsalted butter or nondairy alternative

¼ cup Chambord Raspberry Liqueur

1 pint fresh or frozen raspberries, rinsed

continues

TART CRUST:

▸ Stir the flours, cocoa, sugar, and salt and pour into the bowl of a large food processor. Cut in the butter by pulsing until crumbly. In a separate bowl, beat the egg yolk and ice water together. With the processor running, pour in via the feed tube to bind the pastry dough together. Once mixed and clumped together in a ball, remove the dough from the food processor and work into a flattened disc.

▸ Wrap with foil or plastic wrap and chill until cold.

▸ Preheat the oven to 375°F.

▸ Remove the dough from the refrigerator and press into an oiled pie pan (or 9 x 13 pan if doubling the recipe). The dough will be sticky, so use a rubber spatula or oiled hands to press the dough onto the bottom and lower sides of the pan.

▸ Bake for 20 minutes, remove, and let cool for 10–15 minutes.

TART FILLING:

▸ Using a large food processor, pulse until the chocolate is finely chopped. Set aside without removing the chocolate from the bowl of the food processor.

▸ In a medium saucepan, gradually heat the cream and butter just until boiling. At this point, stir and remove from the heat. Turn the food processor back on while pouring this hot cream mixture through the feed tube, processing until smooth. Pour in the Chambord and process until mixed through.

▸ Spread the berries over the cooled, cooked tart to cover the surface. Pour the chocolate mixture over the top of the berries in the tart. Refrigerate for at least 2 hours, until set. Cut into small pieces and serve chilled on its own or topped with whipped cream (dairy or nondairy alternative).

SERVES 6

5-Minute Chocolate Cake

A similar gluten-full incarnation of this recipe has floated around the Internet and has gained almost mythical status since it enables chocoholics to enjoy homemade chocolate cake in only 5 short minutes! There is no reason those eating gluten-free should be denied such sinful pleasures, so use this recipe in a pinch for company or when you have your own hankering for chocolate cake in a hurry!

1 egg or egg substitute of choice (like Ener-G Egg Replacer or Egg Substitute #1, 3, 4, or 5, page 15)

3 tablespoons canola oil

½ teaspoon vanilla extract, gluten-free

3 tablespoons milk (dairy or nondairy)

4 tablespoons Jules Gluten Free All Purpose Flour (pages 6, 8)

4 tablespoons granulated cane sugar

2 tablespoons unsweetened cocoa

3 tablespoons chocolate chips (dairy or nondairy, e.g., Sunspire or Enjoy Life) (optional)

1 large microwave-safe mug

▸ Whisk the egg, oil, vanilla, and milk together in a very large mug. Add the dry ingredients and mix thoroughly with a small whisk or fork. Add the chocolate chips and stir again.

▸ Place the mug in the microwave and cook for 3 minutes. Microwaves differ in power, so watch for the cake to rise over the top of the mug before removing. The cake will fall a bit as it cools . . . if you can wait that long!

SERVES 1

Chocolate Chip Cookies

Whenever I do a tasting event, this recipe is requested. Folks often do a double-take, thinking that these chewy and delicious cookies could never be gluten-free! This is a great recipe to make and keep as dough in the freezer for a quick dessert, surprise guests, and chocolate-chip-cookie-craving emergencies! Even easier is to use my Jules Gluten Free Chocolate Chip Cookie Mix available at JulesGlutenFree.com.

½ cup butter or nondairy alternative, room temperature

½ cup shortening, room temperature

1 cup brown sugar, firmly packed

½ cup granulated cane sugar

1 teaspoon salt

2 teaspoons vanilla extract, gluten-free

2 large eggs or egg substitute of choice (like Ener-G Egg Replacer or Egg Substitute #1, page 15)

1 teaspoon baking soda

½ teaspoon baking powder, gluten-free

2½ cups Jules Gluten Free All Purpose Flour (pages 6, 8)

8–10 ounces chocolate chips, peanut butter chips (omit if making nut-free), or a mixture thereof (dairy or nondairy, e.g., Sunspire or Enjoy Life)

1½ cups pecans, chopped (optional; omit if making nut-free)

▸ Bring the butter and shortening to room temperature, then beat together until creamy. Cream with sugars, salt, and vanilla, mixing until fluffy. Beat in the eggs, mixing until incorporated. Combine the baking soda, baking powder, and gluten-free flour together; add to wet ingredients and beat until fully mixed. Stir in chips and nuts last, if so desired. Cover the dough and refrigerate or freeze until very cold (this is an important step, so leave enough time in preparation to let the dough chill before baking).

▸ Preheat the oven to 350°F.

▸ Drop the dough by measured teaspoonful onto a parchment-lined or greased cookie sheet, at least 1 inch apart.

▸ Bake for 9–12 minutes, or until the tops are lightly browned (if you like chewier cookies, cook for only 9 minutes). Let them stand 5 minutes before removing them to cooling racks.

MAKES 3 DOZEN COOKIES

See photo insert.

Allergen-Free Chocolate Chip Cookies

These cookies are deliciously crunchy and satisfying, regardless of whether you have any food restrictions. Gluten-free, dairy-free, soy-free, egg-free, and nut-free, you can serve them with confidence to nearly any houseguest. The cookies will not spread during baking, so shape them prior to baking as you want them to look when they are done. There is no need to refrigerate or freeze this dough before baking, and doing so can even dry the dough out a bit since it calls for egg replacer instead of eggs, so try to prepare the dough for baking soon afterward.

> 6 tablespoons butter or nondairy alternative
> 6 tablespoons shortening
> ¾ cup packed light brown sugar
> ½ cup granulated cane sugar
> 2 teaspoons vanilla extract, gluten-free
> 4 teaspoons Ener-G Egg Replacer powder
> 6 tablespoons warm water
> 3 cups Jules Gluten Free All Purpose Flour (pages 6, 8)
> 2 teaspoons gluten-free baking powder
> 1 teaspoon baking soda
> ½ teaspoon salt
> 1¼ cups chocolate chips (dairy or nondairy, e.g., Sunspire or Enjoy Life)

▸ Preheat the oven to 375°F.

▸ Cream the butter, shortening, and sugars until light and fluffy. Add the vanilla.

▸ In a food processor or blender or using a hand mixer, beat together the egg replacer and water at high speed for 1–2 minutes, or until frothy. Add into the sugar mixture and mix well to incorporate.

▸ In another bowl, whisk together the flour, baking powder, baking soda, and salt. Beat into the sugar mixture until combined. Stir in the chips.

▸ Scoop tablespoons of cookie dough onto parchment-lined baking sheets and bake for 12–14 minutes. They will not brown much, so do not wait for browning to remove the cookies. Cook on a wire rack while baking the rest of the batch.

MAKES APPROXIMATELY 3 DOZEN COOKIES

Chocolate Zucchini Cake

It's the end of summer. You have something like fourteen dozen zucchinis left over, just waiting for a recipe like this one. A tricky way to get some vitamins and fiber into your kids' diets—chocolate cake with a purpose!

2½ cups Jules Gluten Free All Purpose Flour (pages 6, 8)

½ cup unsweetened cocoa powder

1 tablespoon baking powder, gluten-free

1½ teaspoons baking soda

½ teaspoon salt

2 teaspoons cinnamon

¾ cup butter or nondairy alternative

1⅔ cups granulated cane sugar

3 large eggs or egg substitute of choice
    (like Ener-G Egg Replacer or two recipes of Egg Substitute #1 or
    2 plus one recipe of Egg Substitute #3, 4, 5, or 6, pages 15–16)

2 teaspoons vanilla extract, gluten-free

2 tablespoons agave nectar or honey

1 tablespoon orange juice or apple cider

2 cups zucchini, coarsely shredded

½ cup milk (dairy or nondairy)

continues

▸ Preheat the oven to 350°F.

▸ Stir together the gluten-free flour, cocoa, baking powder, baking soda, salt, and cinnamon. Set aside.

▸ With an electric mixer beat together the butter and sugar until smoothly blended. Add the eggs one at a time, beating well after each addition, then mix in the vanilla, agave nectar, and orange juice. Fold in the zucchini.

▸ Alternately stir the mixed dry ingredients and the milk into the zucchini mixture.

▸ Pour the batter into a 9- or 10-inch tube pan or bundt pan oiled and lightly dusted with fine gluten-free flour like Jules Gluten Free All Purpose Flour (pages 6, 8) or cornstarch. Fill pan only two-thirds full; pour any remaining batter into oiled ramekins to bake with the larger cake. Bake in the oven for about 50 minutes (test at 45 minutes), or until a cake tester inserted into the center comes out clean. Cool in the pan for 15 minutes; turn out onto a wire rack to cool thoroughly. Once cooled, pour on the glaze and serve.

GLAZE:

2 cups confectioners' sugar
2–3 tablespoons milk (dairy or nondairy)
1 teaspoon vanilla extract, gluten-free

▸ To make the glaze, mix together all the ingredients until smooth. Drizzle the glaze over the cake after it has cooled.

SERVES 8

Coconut Pie

This pie is another family favorite, modified slightly to accommodate various food sensitivities. It is one of my springtime favorites and is so quick and easy because the flour in the pie forms its own crust. Wonderful hot out of the oven, cold, or even at room temperature, I recommend doubling the recipe, because one pie is never enough! Individual ramekins are another great serving alternative as well.

> 1½–2 cups flaked coconut
> 2 cups milk (dairy or nondairy)
> 4 large eggs
> 1½ cups granulated cane sugar
> ½ cup Jules Gluten Free All Purpose Flour (pages 6, 8)
> 1 teaspoon vanilla extract, gluten-free
> 8 tablespoons butter or nondairy alternative, melted

▸ Preheat the oven to 350°F.

▸ Pour the coconut into a small bowl. Add the milk to soak and set aside for at least 10 minutes.

▸ Beat the eggs and sugar then add all the other ingredients slowly. Add the soaked coconut and pour into an oiled pie plate or 4–6 ramekins. This pie rises when cooking, then shrinks as it cools; therefore, use caution not to overfill the pans. I recommend leaving at least an inch clearance to allow for the pie to rise. Consequently, you may find that you have extra pie batter and need to use an additional baking pan.

▸ Bake for 50–60 minutes (approximately 30–40 minutes for ramekins), or until the edges are lightly browned and the middle is no longer jiggly.

SERVES 4–6

Crêpes

Get creative with this recipe: it's great sweet or savory. Fresh fruit, fried bananas or apples, or any other leftovers you want to repurpose . . . the only limitation is your imagination!

Butter or nondairy alternative for the pan
2 tablespoons Jules Gluten Free All Purpose Flour (pages 6, 8)
3 large eggs, slightly beaten
3 tablespoons milk (dairy or nondairy)
½ teaspoon salt

▸ Prepare a small frying pan by heating it to medium-low heat and then adding one tablespoon of butter.

▸ Combine all the crêpe ingredients in a small bowl, mixing until there are no lumps.

▸ When the butter has melted, pour a thin layer of batter onto the pan. Pick up the pan and move it around until all the batter spreads out thinly and begins to set. Cook for only about 1 minute, or until the batter is completely set on the bottom.

▸ Flip the crêpe over gently and cook for only 30 seconds on the other side. Do not burn!

▸ Set crêpe aside, cover, and repeat until all the batter is used. Refresh the butter in the pan as needed to prevent the crêpes from sticking to the pan.

MAKES APPROXIMATELY SIX TO EIGHT 6-INCH CRÊPES

Dark Chocolate Beer Cake

Don't let the name fool you. The dark beer (gluten-free) in this cake subtly enhances the chocolate notes so that this moist and delicious cake is not sickeningly sweet, but rather decadently delicious! This recipe is made on the stovetop, not with a mixer and bowl, so be sure to have a large saucepan ready before starting this recipe.

¾ cup sour cream (dairy or nondairy) or coconut yogurt

2 large eggs or egg substitute of choice (like Ener-G Egg Replacer and Egg Substitute #1, 4, or 5, page 15)

1 tablespoon vanilla extract, gluten-free

1 cup dark beer, gluten-free (e.g., Green's Dubbel Dark Ale)

½ cup unsalted butter or nondairy alternative

¾ cup unsweetened cocoa powder

2 cups granulated sugar

2 cups Jules Gluten Free All Purpose Flour (pages 6, 8)

1 tablespoon baking soda

▸ Preheat the oven to 350°F. Butter or spray with cooking oil a 9-inch springform tube or bundt pan.

▸ In a small bowl, whisk together the sour cream with the eggs and vanilla.

▸ Pour the beer into a large saucepan (drink the rest!). Add the butter and heat just until melted over medium heat. Whisk in the cocoa powder and the sugar until smooth.

▸ Pour the egg mixture into the saucepan mixture and whisk. Add the flour and baking soda until mixed.

▸ Pour into the oiled pan and bake for 35–40 minutes, or until a cake tester inserted into the center of the cake comes out clean. Let the cake cool completely in the pan on a cooling rack and remove from the pan when fully cooled.

▸ Frost the top of the cake with cream cheese frosting or white frosting of choice (see page 177).

Cream Cheese Frosting

8 ounces cream cheese (dairy or nondairy)
1 cup confectioners' sugar
Up to ½ cup heavy cream (dairy or nondairy, like MimicCreme—vegan,
    dairy-, and soy-free but contains nuts)

▸ Whip the cream cheese and sugar until creamy and smooth. Add cream 1 tablespoon at a time and blend to desired consistency. If using nondairy cream and nondairy cream cheese, very little cream is necessary to create a thin icing for this cake.

MAKES APPROXIMATELY 1½ CUPS OF FROSTING

Eggless Cake—White and Chocolate

If you have a special cake occasion and need an egg-free cake, this one's for you! Egg-free cakes work particularly well when baked as cupcakes or in two or more layers, with yummy frosting in between.

4 cups Jules Gluten Free All Purpose Flour (pages 6, 8)

2 tablespoons baking powder, gluten-free

1 teaspoon salt

½ cup unsalted butter or nondairy alternative, softened

1½ cups granulated cane sugar

2 recipes of egg substitute of choice (like Ener-G Egg Replacer or Egg Substitute #1 or 2, page 15)

1¼ cups milk (dairy or nondairy)

(Chocolate Eggless Cake: Add ¼ cup cocoa and increase milk to 1½ cups.)

▸ Preheat the oven to 350°F (static) or 325°F (convection). Spray two 7- or 9-inch round cake pans, three smaller round cake pans or twenty-four cupcake pans with nonstick cooking spray and dust entire surface lightly with gluten-free flour (or line with cupcake papers).

▸ Combine the gluten-free flour, baking powder, and salt and set aside.

▸ Cream the butter and sugar until fluffy, approximately 3 minutes. Add the egg replacer, whipping until incorporated. Gradually mix in the flour mixture, alternating with milk.

▸ Pour the batter into the prepared pan(s). Set aside.

continues

▸ Bake the cakes for 20–30 minutes, depending on the size, turning the pans halfway through if using the convection setting; bake the cupcakes approximately 20 minutes. Before removing from the oven, test for doneness by inserting a cake tester or toothpick in the middle of each cake or into one or more cupcakes to be sure it comes out clean, with no wet crumbs attached. The cakes will also begin to pull away slightly from the sides of the pans when done. Add time if necessary to fully bake.

▸ When done, turn off the oven and leave the oven door open to let the cakes cool slowly for 10 minutes or so, then remove the cake pans to a cooling rack. After 20–30 minutes of total cooling time, gently invert the cakes in their pans to remove them, then flip gently back onto the cooling rack until fully cooled. Frost the cakes only when fully cooled, or in the alternative, wrap the cooled cakes with wax paper or plastic wrap, then seal inside freezer bags to freeze or refrigerate until ready to use.

SERVES 8–10

(For frosting options, see pages 177–178, 188, 190, 203.)

Fresh Fruit Crumble

Make this recipe with a budding baker in your house, or even just a kid who is bored and easily impressed. This recipe is hard to mess up and the rewards are priceless.

1½ cups blueberries, blackberries, raspberries, or other fresh berries
7 peaches, peeled and sliced thinly
3 tablespoons granulated cane sugar
1 tablespoon cinnamon
2/3 cup rolled oats, certified gluten-free
¼ cup cream of buckwheat (100 percent buckwheat)
1/3 cup pecans, chopped (optional; omit if making nut-free)
3 tablespoons butter or nondairy alternative, melted

▸ Preheat the oven to 350°F (static) or 325°F (convection).

▸ Prepare a 9 x 13-inch pan by lightly coating with cooking oil.

▸ Wash and stir all prepared fruit together with 1 tablespoon sugar in the baking pan. Set aside.

▸ Whisk the dry ingredients together in a large mixing bowl, along with the remaining 2 tablespoons of sugar and cinnamon. Stir in the melted butter until a crumble is formed. Sprinkle evenly over the fruit mixture in the pan.

▸ Bake for 30 minutes, or until the crumble is crispy. Cool slightly and serve plain or with vanilla yogurt (dairy or nondairy) or ice cream on top.

SERVES 6

Fruit Crisp

Crisps are easy but memorable desserts. Find what's ripe locally and have at it. Then repeat the process as other seasonal fruits become available.

¼–½ cup granulated cane sugar

4 cups fruit (apples, peaches, plums, berries, etc.), peeled, rinsed, and chopped

½ cup Jules Gluten Free All Purpose Flour (pages 6, 8)

1½ cups oats, certified gluten-free

½ cup brown sugar

1½ teaspoons cinnamon

8 tablespoons cold butter or nondairy alternative

½ teaspoon almond extract, gluten-free (if using peaches)

▸ Preheat the oven to 400°F (static) or 375°F (convection).

▸ In a large bowl, add sugar to the fruit, to taste, and pour into an ungreased 8 x 8-inch baking pan. Set aside to allow the sugar to encourage syrup to form.

▸ In another bowl, combine gluten-free flour with the oats, brown sugar, and cinnamon. Cut in the butter with a fork or pastry cutter until the mixture becomes a rough crumble. Crumble the mixture over the fruit in the baking pan. Bake in a preheated oven for 30 minutes, or until the topping is light brown and crispy.

▸ Serve warm with ice cream or whipped cream.

SERVES 6

Fudge

Don't shy away from trying this recipe just because of the mystique that comes with making candy. This fudge is so easy that it is cooked in a microwave and you don't even need a candy thermometer! A handy rule of thumb with fudge: if it has not cooked long enough or at high enough heat, it will be very soft when cooled; if it cooked too long or at too high a temperature, it will be very hard when cooled. The fudge will still taste good either way, but take note for the next time you make the recipe, in the event you prefer your fudge softer or harder than it turns out the first time you make it.

3 cups granulated cane sugar

¾ cup butter or nondairy alternative

5 ounces evaporated milk (dairy or nondairy, page 19)

12 ounces chocolate chips (dairy or nondairy, e.g., Sunspire or Enjoy Life)

1 (7-ounce) jar marshmallow cream*

1 teaspoon vanilla extract, gluten-free

1 cup chopped nuts (optional)

continues

---

* Marshmallow Crème and Marshmallow Fluff contain egg whites; Ricemellow Crème is vegan (egg-free) but contains soy. Check product ingredients prior to use to be sure they meet your dietary needs.

▸ Place sugar, butter, and evaporated milk in a very large microwave-safe bowl and microwave on high heat until melted. Stir, then microwave until the mixture comes to a full rolling boil. Without turning the microwave off or opening the door, add 5 minutes of boiling time to the mixture.

▸ Meanwhile, oil or butter a 9 x 13-inch baking pan. Open the jar of marshmallow cream and the bag of chocolate chips so that they are ready to add immediately after the boiling process.

▸ Remove the boiling mixture from the microwave (the bowl may be hot!), and add the chips and marshmallow cream with a rubber or silicone spatula; stir vigorously to mix. Add vanilla and nuts, if you choose, then use a mixer to beat the mixture until smooth. Quickly pour into the prepared pan and smooth using the spatula. Add any toppings (like crushed candy canes) you desire at this point, then set aside to cool.

▸ Do not cut until the fudge has cooled.

SERVES 10

Gingerbread Men/Gingersnap Cookies

This is one of my all-time favorite recipes, and one you can share it with nearly anyone, as it is virtually allergen-free! Get creative with the decorations if making into gingerbread men, using colored sugar, red hot candies, peppermint, frosting, or fancy cookie cutters! For an even easier recipe, just use my Jules Gluten Free Gingersnap Mix available at JulesGlutenFree.com.

¾ cup butter or nondairy alternative
¼ cup molasses or dark agave nectar
1 cup brown sugar
1 teaspoon vanilla extract, gluten-free
1½ cups Jules Gluten Free All Purpose Flour (pages 6, 8)
1 cup fine white rice flour
½ cup buckwheat or brown rice flour
Dash of salt
2 teaspoons cinnamon
2 teaspoons ginger
1 teaspoon cloves
3 teaspoons baking powder, gluten-free
½ cup water

▸ Beat together the first four ingredients in one large bowl and whisk together all of the remaining ingredients except the water in another bowl. Slowly stir the dry mixture into the first bowl, adding water as necessary to create a consistency such that you could make a ball with the dough. Divide the dough in half and refrigerate until very cold, at least two hours.

▸ Preheat the oven to 325°F (static) or 300°F (convection).

continues

GINGERBREAD MEN:

▸ Roll one-half the dough out onto a surface dusted with gluten-free flour. The dough should make a large ¼-inch thick rectangle. You may roll it more thinly or more thickly, depending on how you prefer your cookies: the thinner the dough, the crispier the cookie. Cut into cookies and lift with a spatula onto a parchment-lined baking sheet.

▸ Bake for 25–30 minutes, or until they are lightly browned. Let cool on the baking sheet 5 minutes before transferring to a cooling rack.

GINGERSNAP COOKIES:

▸ Roll teaspoon-size balls of dough gently between your palms (the dough will be sticky), then place on parchment-lined baking sheets.

▸ Bake for 15 minutes. Remove and sprinkle lightly with demerara or coarsely granulated cane sugar.

MAKES 3–4 DOZEN COOKIES, DEPENDING ON THE SIZE

Graham Crackers

Not only does this cookie taste good by itself, but it allows us non—graham eaters to actually enjoy a graham-like cracker crust! Sprinkle sugar and cinnamon on top before baking for variety and get ready for s'mores again! For another fun option, roll the dough to ¼-inch thick and cut to the size of an ice cream sandwich, bake, and cool. Then pick your favorite ice cream or nondairy substitute, place a scoop between two cookies, wrap tightly in plastic wrap, and freeze for an allergen-free ice cream sandwich to enjoy on any hot summer day! For an even easier recipe, try my Jules Gluten Free Graham Cracker Mix available at JulesGlutenFree.com.

> ¾ cup butter or nondairy alternative
> ¼ cup honey or 3 tablespoons light agave nectar
> 1 cup brown sugar
> 1 teaspoon vanilla extract, gluten-free
> 1½ cups Jules Gluten Free All Purpose Flour (pages 6, 8)
> 1 cup fine white rice flour
> ½ cup buckwheat or brown rice flour
> Dash of salt
> 2 teaspoons cinnamon
> 3 teaspoons baking powder, gluten-free
> ½ cup cold water
> Cinnamon-sugar mixture for topping

▸ Beat together the first four ingredients in one large bowl and mix all of the remaining dry ingredients in another bowl. Slowly stir the dry mixture into the first bowl, adding water as necessary to create a consistency such that you could make a ball with the dough.

▸ Divide the dough in half, cover, and refrigerate for two hours or until very cold.

continues

‣ Preheat the oven to 325°F (static) or 300°F (convection).

‣ Roll one half of the dough out onto a surface floured with gluten-free flour. The dough should make a large rectangle ⅛- to ¼-inch thick. You may roll it more thinly or more thickly, depending on how you prefer your cookies: the thinner the dough, the crispier the cookie.

‣ Cut into small rectangles like graham crackers and lift with a spatula onto a baking sheet lined with parchment paper. Finally, prick each cracker with a fork in rows, as you would with a graham cracker. Sprinkle with cinnamon-sugar mixture, if desired.

‣ Bake for 20–30 minutes, or until they are lightly browned. Let them cool on the baking sheet 5 minutes before lifting to a cooling rack.

MAKES 4–5 DOZEN GRAHAM CRACKERS, DEPENDING ON SIZE

Key Lime Pie

I'd like to thank the person who came up with the first key lime pie recipe—truly the taste of summer in the shape of a pie. Your family and friends and guests will thank you for this version, too! Light, refreshing . . . just like you remember.

GRAHAM CRACKER PIE CRUST:

1 cup Graham Crackers, gluten-free (see page 212), chopped until finely crumbled

⅔ cup almonds, chopped finely (nut-free option: use additional ⅔ cup graham crackers)

¼ cup granulated cane sugar

4–5 tablespoons butter or nondairy alternative, melted

FILLING:

2 tablespoons Jules Gluten Free All Purpose Flour (pages 6, 8)

3 large eggs

1¼ cups milk (dairy or nondairy)

¾ cup granulated cane sugar

½ cup firm tofu or cream cheese (dairy or nondairy)

½ cup key lime juice

2 tablespoons lime zest

1 teaspoon vanilla extract, gluten-free

MERINGUE:

3 large egg whites

½ teaspoon lime juice

6 tablespoons granulated cane sugar

continues

CRUST:

▸ Preheat the oven to 350°F.

▸ Chop the crackers and almonds, if using, in a food processor until fine. Once uniformly crushed, measure out to be sure you have 1⅔ cups of crumbs—repeat if you need more crumbs.

▸ Pour the sugar into the food processor with the crumbs and pulse until integrated. Add in the melted butter, pulsing until the crumbs begin to stick together. If you find you need slightly more butter to get the crumbs to hold together, melt an additional tablespoon and add it in the same way.

▸ Pour the crumb-butter mixture into a pie pan and press with your fingers to create an even thickness along the bottom and sides of the pan. Bake in preheated oven for 10 minutes—do not allow the edges to burn, though. Remove and set aside until the pie filling is prepared.

FILLING:

▸ Combine all the ingredients in a large food processor or mixer and process or beat until smooth. Pour into the cooked crust and bake for 40 minutes. If the crust edges are browning too much, cover with a pie crust saver or aluminum foil. Set the baked pie aside to cool for 2 hours and serve plain or with Berry Coulis (page 175), or prepare with meringue topping according to meringue directions below.

MERINGUE:

▸ Separate the egg yolks and egg whites—discard the yolks and save the whites in a separate bowl (be sure there is no yolk at all in the bowl with the egg whites). Beat the egg whites in a clean metal bowl with clean whisk attachments to your mixer until the whites are foamy. Add the lime juice and continue beating on high until peaks begin to form. Add the sugar in gradually while beating, and whip until the mixture is stiff.

▸ When the pie is done baking, remove from the oven and swirl the meringue over the top of the pie, spreading to touch the outer edges of the pie pan, covering the entire pie.

▸ Return to the oven and bake until the meringue tips are light brown, approximately 10–15 minutes.

▸ Remove from the oven to a cooling rack and cool for 2 hours before slicing.

SERVES 6–8

Lemon Bars

Ever a favorite, no matter what time of year, these light and fresh bars can't help but bring a smile to your face. They're like sunshine . . . on a cookie!

CRUST:

⅓ cup (5⅓ tablespoons) butter or nondairy alternative

¼ cup granulated cane sugar

1 cup Jules Gluten Free All Purpose Flour (pages 6, 8)

FILLING:

2 eggs or egg substitute of choice (like Egg Substitute #5, page 15)

¾ cup granulated cane sugar

2 tablespoons Jules Gluten Free All Purpose Flour

2 teaspoons finely shredded lemon peel

3 tablespoons lemon juice

¼ teaspoon gluten-free baking powder

Confectioners' sugar (optional)

▸ Preheat the oven to 350°F (static).

CRUST:

▸ In a medium bowl, beat butter with a mixer on medium to high speed for 30 seconds. Add the ¼ cup of sugar; beat until combined. Beat in the 1 cup of flour until crumbly, being careful not to overmix. Press the mixture into the bottom of an un-oiled 8 x 8 x 2-inch baking pan. Bake for 15 minutes or until golden.

FILLING:

▸ Combine eggs, sugar, flour, lemon peel, lemon juice, and baking powder; beat 2 minutes or until thoroughly combined.

▸ Pour the filling over the baked crust. Bake 20 minutes more or until set and lightly browned. Cool on a wire rack. Cut into bars only when completely cool. Sprinkle with confectioners' sugar, if desired, before serving.

MAKES 20 BARS.

THIS RECIPE DOUBLES NICELY WHEN BAKED IN A 9 X 13-INCH PAN.

See photo insert.

Magic Bar Cookies

These bar cookies have been a favorite in my family for generations (my Grandma called them "Hello Dollies"), but they are so much more than just cookies. They are "empty-your-pantry, suit-your-taste, won't-last-one-day-in-your-house" bars! I give you some suggested ingredients and proportions in my recipe below, but don't hesitate to tailor these bars to what you have on hand and what you want in your mouth! Chocolate chips, peanut butter chips, pecans, coconut, oats—whatever you want to layer on these bars, just don't forget the graham crackers and the sweetened condensed milk (dairy or nondairy) that seal the deal and hold these bars together.

½ cup butter or nondairy alternative

1½ cups gluten-free graham crackers, crushed
   (or Graham Crackers, page 212, then crush baked grahams)

1 cup flaked coconut

½ cup certified gluten-free oats

1½ cups chocolate chips, peanut butter chips
   (omit if making nut-free), or a combination, dairy or nondairy
   (e.g., Sunspire or Enjoy Life dairy-free chips)

½ cup chopped pecans (optional; omit if making nut-free)

14 ounces sweetened condensed milk (dairy or nondairy, page 20)

▶ Preheat the oven to 350°F (static) or 325°F (convection).

▶ Spray a 9 x 13-inch pan with cooking oil, then melt butter in the pan, either on the stove, in the oven, or if in a glass pan, in the microwave. Pour the crumbs into the pan on top of the melted butter, but do not stir. Layer the remaining ingredients in the following order: coconut; oats; chocolate chips; nuts. Finally, pour the sweetened, condensed milk over the bars in a lattice pattern. Ultimately, this will fill in over the whole pan.

▶ Bake for 25–30 minutes, just until the milk has turned a light brown color. Allow to cool before cutting bars.

Nut Butter Cookies

They're not only melt-in-your mouth delicious but also gluten-free, dairy-free, egg-free, soy-free, and can be made nut-free and even sugar-free! Enjoy these cookies on their own, or add dairy-free chocolate chips for a change of pace. High protein, loads of vitamins and minerals, dietary fiber—it's all there . . . and in a cookie! Maybe I should have called these "Guilt-Free Cookies"!

Don't be daunted by some of the unusual flour ingredients. I experiment with them once in a while for added protein or fiber. Try them if you will, or simply use my all-purpose blend instead, for a quick and easy recipe substitution. If using a peanut butter alternative, additional flour may be necessary to stiffen the dough—add one tablespoon at a time until the dough holds together in a ball.

1½ cups peanut butter, soy "nut" butter, or sunflower "nut" butter

¾ cup agave nectar (light or dark or use honey)

1 tablespoon vanilla extract, gluten-free

¼ cup unsweetened applesauce

½ teaspoon salt

1 cup Jules Gluten Free All Purpose Flour (pages 6, 8)

¾ cup buckwheat flour (or Jules Gluten Free All Purpose Flour)

4 tablespoons almond meal or buckwheat flour, brown rice flour, gluten-free oat flour, or Jules Gluten Free All Purpose Flour

½ cup (or more) chocolate chips, optional (dairy or nondairy, e.g., Sunspire or Enjoy Life)

Granulated cane sugar, granulated Splenda or cinnamon for tops of cookies

▶ Preheat the oven to 350°F (static) or 325°F (convection).

▶ Blend "nut" butter and all liquid ingredients together, then add in the dry ingredients, mixing until fully incorporated.

▶ Prepare a cookie sheet lined with parchment paper. Roll balls of dough no larger than the size of ping pong balls in your hands, and place on the prepared cookie sheet. Dip a fork in the sugar, Splenda, or cinnamon and press into each cookie to flatten with a crisscross design.

▶ Bake for 10–12 minutes and remove from the oven to cool on the pan before lifting to a plate.

MAKES APPROXIMATELY 2 DOZEN COOKIES

Nut Butter and Jelly Cookies

Jelly makes for a simple, delicious, and dare I say, logical addition, to the fabled peanut-butter cookie.

⅓ cup smooth peanut butter, almond or cashew butters (if avoiding only peanuts), soy "nut" butter, or sunflower "nut" butter

¼ cup granulated cane sugar

½ cup brown sugar

3 tablespoons shortening, room temperature

¼ cup unsweetened applesauce

1 large egg or egg substitute of choice (like Ener-G egg replacer or Egg Substitute #7, page 16)

1½ cups Jules Gluten Free All Purpose Flour (pages 6, 8) (you may need ¼–½ cup additional flour if using alternative nut butters)

2 tablespoons or less water

Preserves, jelly, or jam

▸ Preheat the oven to 350°F (static) or 325°F (convection).

▸ Mix the nut butter and sugars together in a medium-size mixing bowl until smooth. Add the shortening, applesauce, and egg, then the dry ingredients, mixing well. If using alternative nut butters or "natural" peanut butter, and the dough is very sticky or runny, mix in an additional ¼–½ cup of Jules Gluten Free All Purpose Flour, adding flour gradually until the dough holds together in a ball. Add water as necessary for the dough to hold together without being crumbly.

▸ Spoon out tablespoon-size portions, roll between your palms and place onto parchment-lined or ungreased cookie sheets. Leave about 1 inch between each cookie to allow for spread.

▸ Press your thumb straight down into the middle of each cookie, but not all the way to the pan, leaving a dimpled impression, then spoon a small amount of preserves into the center of each cookie; try not to let any drip outside of the dimple.

▸ Bake for 10 minutes or until they are lightly browned.

MAKES 2 DOZEN COOKIES

Oatmeal Raisin Cookies

Uncontaminated, certified gluten-free oats can be a wonderful complement to a gluten-free diet. The nutritional benefits oats offer—like adding beneficial dietary fiber and protein—combined with the opportunity to enjoy comfort foods like oatmeal and oatmeal raisin cookies again, have made oats one of my favorite grains. If you would like to learn more about integrating oats into a gluten-free diet, check out *The First Year: Celiac Disease and Living Gluten-Free.*

For those of you who find you are unable to give gluten-free oats a go, try this recipe with rice flakes or quinoa flakes instead. This recipe produces moist, chewy, cinnamon-y cookies that are hard to turn down. I've offered a dairy-free and even egg-free option, so there are even more reasons to try it!

½ cup granulated cane sugar

½ cup light brown sugar

½ cup butter or nondairy alternative

2 eggs or egg substitute of choice
(like Ener-G Egg Replacer or
Egg Substitute #1 or 2, page 15)

2 teaspoons vanilla extract, gluten-free

1¼ cups Jules Gluten Free All Purpose
Flour (pages 6, 8)

½ teaspoon baking soda

2 teaspoons baking powder,
gluten-free

¼ teaspoon salt

1 tablespoon cinnamon

1½ cups oats, certified gluten-free

½ cup baking raisins (or raisins
boiled, then drained before
baking)

▸ Cream the sugars and butter until light and fluffy. Add the eggs one at a time and thoroughly incorporate into the batter. Stir in the vanilla last.

▸ In a separate bowl, whisk together all dry ingredients (except oats), mixing well. Gradually stir into the creamed mixture until integrated. Add in the oats and raisins. Mix until fully integrated, then cover tightly and refrigerate for 2 hours or until cold.

▸ Preheat the oven to 350°F (static) or 325°F (convection).

▸ Roll the dough into tablespoon-size balls and place at least 2 inches apart on a parchment-lined cookie sheet. Bake for 8–10 minutes, or until light brown. Let them cool on a wire rack before removing.

MAKES 2–3 DOZEN COOKIES

Pecan Sandies

Most of my recipes requiring flour use my all-purpose flour mixture as the only flour because I try to avoid the expense and frustration of multiple gluten-free flours in different recipes. Every so often though, a recipe comes along that requires something my flour mixture doesn't have—grit. Recipes like graham crackers and pecan sandies are supposed to be gritty, so we have to resort to adding gritty rice flour to create that classic taste. You can make this recipe without running to the store to get rice flour, but expect a smoother-tasting cookie. If avoiding tree nuts, go with the flaxseed substitution described for a nutty taste, but without the chunks of pecans.

¾ cup butter or nondairy alternative, room temperature

½ cup brown sugar, packed

1 teaspoon vanilla extract, gluten-free

2 tablespoons vanilla yogurt (dairy or nondairy)

1 large egg or egg substitute of choice (like Ener-G Egg Replacer or Egg Substitute #1 or 2, page 15)

¾ cup Jules Gluten Free All Purpose Flour (pages 6, 8)

¼ cup white rice flour

1 cup pecans, finely chopped (or ½ cup coarsely ground flaxseed plus up to ¼ cup additional yogurt for tree nut–free option)

▸ Cream the butter and brown sugar in a large bowl until light and fluffy. Add the vanilla, yogurt, and egg, beating until light and thoroughly mixed. Finally, mix in the flours and pecans or flaxseed meal. If using flaxseed meal, add up to ¼ cup additional yogurt until the dough is not crumbly.

▸ Refrigerate the dough until cold, at least 1–2 hours.

▸ Preheat the oven to 350°F (static) or 325°F (convection).

▸ Scoop tablespoons of the dough onto a parchment-lined baking sheet, flattening the balls of dough slightly. The final product will look very much coming out of the oven like it did going in, so make it pretty!

▸ Bake for 10–15 minutes, until cooked through and slightly browned. Cool for 5 minutes before removing from baking sheet.

MAKES 2 DOZEN COOKIES

My Grandma's Pie Crust

This is literally my grandma's famous flaky pie crust with only one substitution . . . the flour! The recipe makes one 8- or 9-inch pie crust; double amounts for a two-crust pie. I used to recommend refrigerating this crust before rolling, but I've learned through much trial and error that it is actually much easier to work with if the dough is allowed to rest at room temperature for about 30 minutes before rolling out. You can refrigerate or freeze it at that point by covering tightly with plastic wrap and then aluminum foil, or simply add your fillings and bake.

> 1 cup Jules Gluten Free All Purpose Flour (pages 6, 8)
> ½ teaspoon salt
> ⅓ cup shortening or butter or nondairy alternative (works best to use at least half shortening, remaining portion butter or nondairy alternative)
> 2–3 tablespoons cold water
> Milk (dairy or nondairy) for brushing on crust before baking

▸ In a large bowl, whisk together the flour and salt. Cut in the shortening and/or butter using two knives or a pastry cutter until it resembles a fine meal (this step is even easier if using a food processor instead).

▸ Add the water gradually to make the consistency you need to form a ball—err on the side of it being wetter rather than crumbly. Form a ball with the dough, press lightly between your hands to form it into a disc, and wrap in plastic. Set aside on the counter at room temperature for 30 minutes while you make your filling.

▸ After allowing the dough to rest, roll the pastry out onto a surface dusted with fine gluten-free flour like Jules Gluten Free All Purpose Flour (pages 6, 8) or cornstarch. A flexible pastry sheet (e.g., Silpat) for that purpose works well. Roll the disc to a diameter at least 1 inch larger than the diameter of your pie pan.

▸ Using a pastry blade or butter knife, gently lift an edge of the rolled out crust over your rolling pin and use the pin to help support the crust while lifting it onto the pie plate. Once in the pie plate, gently pat into shape and fill with your desired filling. Fill any cracks in the crust with extra pieces of crust by wetting the crust and gently pressing the crust pieces together.

continues

- For a two-crust pie like an apple pie, double the ingredients and divide the doubled pie crust before setting aside and wrapping each equal ball of dough in plastic wrap. Repeat the rolling-out steps and lay the crust gently onto the top of the filled pie pan. Cut off all but ½–1 inch of excess pie crust from around the edge of the pan. For fruit pies, cut small slits in the center of the top crust to allow the hot steam to escape.

- If there are any tears in your top crust, never fear! Simply take leftover crust and use decorative cookie cutters to cut out leaves, pumpkins, etc.; wet the backside of each cutout with a dab of milk or water; then lay on top of any tears to cover the flaw. Fold approximately ½ inch of excess pie crust all around the edge to form the crust, then using your fingers, press a fluted design in the crust to finish or press with the floured tines of a fork all around the crust edges to decoratively seal.

- Cover crust edges with foil or a pie crust saver to minimize burning. Remove the foil with 10 minutes left of baking and brush the crust with your milk of choice or egg whites—this step helps it to brown nicely. Repeat brushing the crust every 15–20 minutes of bake time.

- Single crust pie: Preheat the oven to 375°F (static) and bake for 35 to 40 minutes, or follow directions specific to the pie recipe.

- Double-crust pie: Preheat the oven to 400°F (static) and bake for 40 minutes, remove the foil, and bake for another 10–20 minutes or until the juices are bubbling, or follow directions specific to your particular pie recipe.

MAKES 1 PIE CRUST

Pumpkin-Chip Bars

Pumpkin is such a wonderful ingredient: not only does it add flavor to so many different types of foods, but it can actually be used to replace eggs in most any recipe! Here, I use it with my base recipe for chocolate chip cookies, allowing me to reduce the eggs by one.

2 cups Jules Gluten Free All Purpose Flour (pages 6, 8)

1 tablespoon pumpkin pie spice (or ½ teaspoon ground cloves, 1½ teaspoons cinnamon, and 1 teaspoon nutmeg)

1 teaspoon baking soda

½ teaspoon baking powder, gluten-free

1 cup butter or nondairy alternative

1¼ cups granulated sugar

1 large egg or egg substitute of choice (like Ener-G Egg Replacer or Egg Substitute #1 or 2, page 15)

2 teaspoons vanilla extract, gluten-free

15 ounces pumpkin puree

6 ounces chocolate chips (dairy or nondairy, e.g., Sunspire or Enjoy Life)

▸ Preheat the oven to 350°F.

▸ Line a 9 x 13-inch baking pan with parchment paper, covering the bottom and sides.

▸ Whisk together the flour, spices, baking soda, and baking powder and set aside.

▸ In a large mixing bowl, beat together the butter and sugar on high speed until fluffy. Add the egg and vanilla, mixing well. Finally, add the pumpkin. When fully integrated, pour in the dry ingredients slowly, mixing on low until combined. Stir in the chocolate chips last.

▸ Pour the batter into the prepared baking pan and spread with a rubber spatula until smooth. Bake for 35 minutes, or until a cake tester inserted into the center of the bars comes out clean.

▸ Cool on a wire rack and when removing the bars, simply lift the parchment paper and transfer to a platter or large plate to cut and serve. These are wonderful served warm with vanilla ice cream or yogurt on top!

MAKES 12–24 BARS

Pumpkin Cookies

Looking at the ingredients for these, you'd think they were little pumpkin pies! They're definitely Fall-ish, definitely pumpkin-ish, and have some of the spices that make them taste pie-ish. But they really deserve their own description. Pumpkin—the new chocolate?!

COOKIE:

2½ cups Jules Gluten Free All Purpose Flour (pages 6, 8)

2 teaspoons baking powder, gluten-free

½ teaspoon baking soda

2 teaspoons ground cinnamon

1 teaspoon ground nutmeg

½ teaspoon ground cloves

½ teaspoon salt

½ cup granulated cane sugar

½ cup brown sugar

½ cup butter or nondairy alternative

1 cup pumpkin puree

1 large egg or egg substitute of choice (like Ener-G Egg Replacer or Egg Substitute #1 or 2, page 15)

1 teaspoon vanilla extract, gluten-free

¼ cup molasses

ICING:

1 cup confectioners' sugar

2 tablespoons milk (dairy or nondairy)

½ teaspoon vanilla extract, gluten-free

▸ Whisk together all the dry ingredients except the sugars in a large bowl and set aside.

▸ Using an electric mixer, cream the sugars and butter until fluffy. Add the pumpkin, egg, vanilla, and molasses, beating until creamed. Stir in the dry ingredients until combined. Wrap tightly with plastic wrap and refrigerate until the dough is chilled.

▸ Preheat the oven to 350°F (static) or 325°F (convection).

▸ Prepare a cookie sheet by covering with parchment paper. Drop the cookies by rounded tablespoons onto the parchment paper. Bake for 15–20 minutes, or until they resist sinking when lightly touched with a finger.

▸ Set the cookies aside to cool while preparing the icing by stirring the ingredients together in a small bowl until all the lumps are incorporated. When the cookies are cooled, drizzle the glaze onto the tops of the cookies in a crisscross pattern or over the entire tops with a spoon.

MAKES 2–3 DOZEN COOKIES

Pumpkin Pie

I love making pumpkin pies. And I love watching how truly those who love them, love them. Is anything more autumnal than a pumpkin pie? If you've been avoiding them because you're eating dairy-free, you're in luck. For a delicious egg-free pumpkin pie, opt for my crustless version, page 227. Make any day Thanksgiving with this recipe—another reason to give thanks.

1 recipe of My Grandma's Pie Crust (see page 222)

15 ounces pumpkin puree

1 cup milk (dairy or nondairy vanilla flavor)

2 tablespoons butter or nondairy alternative, melted

3 tablespoons bourbon or spiced apple cider

1 tablespoon lemon juice

2 large eggs

2 tablespoons Jules Gluten Free All Purpose Flour (pages 6, 8)

½ cup brown sugar, packed

¼ cup granulated cane sugar

½ teaspoon sea salt

2 teaspoons cinnamon

2 teaspoons pumpkin pie spice (or 1½ teaspoons nutmeg plus ½ teaspoon cloves)

▸ Preheat the oven to 450°F.

▸ Butter or spray with cooking oil a 10-inch pie plate and one oiled ramekin.

▸ Prepare the pie crust.

▸ Mix together all the liquid ingredients in one bowl and whisk together the dry ingredients in another. Slowly pour the dry ingredients in to the liquid bowl while stirring. Beat until totally combined.

▸ Pour the mixture into the unbaked pie crust, leaving at least ¼ inch between the batter and the top of the crust. Pour any remaining batter into prepared ramekin(s). Smooth the top of the pie with a rubber spatula.

▸ Bake at 450°F for 15 minutes, then reduce the heat to 375°F and bake for 30 more minutes or until a knife inserted into the pie comes out clean.

SERVES 6–8

Pumpkin Pie (Crustless)

If you think that you have to skip pumpkin pie because . . .

a) you're not confident yet at making a gluten-free pie crust,
b) you think you don't have time to make a homemade crust and everything else,
c) you are contending with food allergies, or
d) all of the above

. . . think again! This recipe solves all of these problems and is totally delicious. Easy, quick, and practically allergen-free, you'll want to keep this recipe handy for more than just Thanksgiving! Of course, if you really like your pie crust, feel free to use this recipe with a pie crust (see page 222).

15 ounces pumpkin puree
¾ cup milk (dairy or nondairy vanilla flavor)
¾ cup cream or liquid vanilla creamer (nondairy)
2 tablespoons extra-virgin olive oil
2 teaspoons vanilla extract, gluten-free
4 tablespoons bourbon (use only if using egg replacer)
½ cup Jules Gluten Free All Purpose Flour (pages 6, 8)
¼ cup buckwheat flour
½ cup brown sugar, packed
¼ cup granulated cane sugar
1 tablespoon Ener-G Egg Replacer powder—not reconstituted
   (or use 2 whole large eggs and no bourbon)
2 teaspoons baking powder, gluten-free
½ teaspoon sea salt
2 teaspoons cinnamon
1 teaspoon pumpkin pie spice (or ¾ teaspoon nutmeg plus
   ¼ teaspoon cloves)

continues

▸ Preheat the oven to 450°F.

▸ Butter or spray with cooking oil a 10-inch pie plate and one ramekin.

▸ Mix together all the liquid ingredients in one bowl and whisk together the dry ingredients in another. Slowly pour the dry ingredients in to the liquid bowl while stirring. Beat until totally combined.

▸ Pour into the prepared pie plate, leaving at least ¼ inch between the batter and the rim of the pie plate.

▸ Pour any remaining batter into prepared ramekin(s). Smooth the top of the pie with a rubber spatula.

▸ Bake at 450°F for 15 minutes, then reduce the heat to 375°F and bake for 30 more minutes or until a knife inserted into the pie comes out clean.

SERVES 6–8

Shortcakes

You'll want to have some fresh berries at the ready when you make these delicious little cakes—they soak up the juices from the berries and transform into an even more delightful treat. Try topping with a dollop of yogurt on the berries and you can even serve them for breakfast!

2 cups Jules Gluten Free All Purpose Flour (pages 6, 8)

¼ cup granulated cane sugar

2 teaspoons baking powder, gluten-free

½ teaspoon baking soda

4 tablespoons shortening

2 large eggs or egg substitute of choice (like Ener-G Egg Replacer or Egg Substitute #1, 2, or 7, pages 15–16), mixed

¾ cup vanilla yogurt (dairy or nondairy)

Butter or nondairy alternative to brush on top

Cinnamon-sugar mixture
   (3 tablespoons sugar plus ½ teaspoon cinnamon)

Chopped berries for topping

▸ Preheat the oven to 400°F.

▸ Mix together all the dry ingredients in a large bowl. Cut the shortening into the dry ingredients using a pastry cutter or food processor. Add the eggs and yogurt and stir well until combined.

▸ Pat the dough out onto a surface dusted with fine gluten-free flour (like Jules Gluten Free All Purpose Flour, pages 6, 8, or cornstarch) to a thickness of about 1 inch. Cut into circles or other shapes with biscuit cutters or the rim of a drinking glass (do not twist when cutting). Gather up the dough not already cut into shapes and re-pat and re-cut until all the dough is used. Place shortcakes onto a parchment-lined cookie sheet. Brush the tops of each short-cake with butter or nondairy alternative and sprinkle with the premade cinnamon-sugar mixture described in the recipe above.

▸ Bake for 8–10 minutes, or just until the tops are lightly browned. Do not overbake! Serve with fresh berries, ice cream, or yogurt.

MAKES APPROXIMATELY 18 LARGE SHORTCAKES

See photo insert.

Strawberry-Fig Pie

If you want a slightly offbeat and truly healthy ending to a meal, this pie will satisfy that need, and your sweet tooth.

CRUST:

1½ cups pecans, finely chopped

1¼ cups dried figs or dates, chopped

1 teaspoon vanilla extract, gluten-free

(or you may use 1 recipe traditional pie crust, page 222)

PIE FILLING:

1 cup dried figs or dates, chopped

1½ bananas, ripe and mashed

2 tablespoons light agave nectar or honey

¼ cup Jules Gluten Free All Purpose Flour (pages 6, 8)

2½ cups strawberries, coarsely chopped
   (or 2 cups strawberries plus ½ cup blueberries)

¼ cup strawberries, sliced

▸ Preheat the oven to 350°F.

▸ Prepare the crust ingredients by chopping the pecans in a food processor, then adding the dried fruit and chopping together. Finally, pour in the vanilla and blend them all together in the food processor.

▸ Press the mixture into the bottom and sides of a pie plate and set aside. In the alternative, prepare a traditional pie crust according to recipe instructions, page 222.

▸ Clean the blade and bowl of your food processor and add the figs or dates, bananas, agave, and flour. Combine until well mixed and pour into a large bowl. Stir in the chopped strawberries, then pour the mixture into the prepared crust. Top with sliced strawberries.

▸ Bake in the preheated oven for 20–30 minutes, or until the pie begins to be slightly bubbly in the center. Remove to cool and refrigerate until serving.

SERVES 6

Strawberry Pie

You may either use a baked traditional pie crust (see page 222) or a graham cracker crust (see page 214) to prepare this yummy and totally easy dessert.

> 3 pints fresh strawberries (may use frozen)
> ¾ cup granulated cane sugar
> 3 tablespoons cornstarch
> 1 tablespoon lemon juice
> ½ teaspoon Grand Marnier (or orange juice)
> 1 gluten-free pie crust (page 222 or page 214)

▸ Place half of the strawberries into a large stovetop pan and mash, adding the sugar and cornstarch to the mixture. Cook over low heat, stirring to prevent from burning for at least 5 minutes until thickened. Slowly add the lemon juice and Grand Marnier. Remove from the heat and let the mixture cool.

▸ Cut the remaining berries to bite-size pieces and add gently to the mixture. Pour into the prepared pie crust and refrigerate before serving. Top with yogurt, whipped cream, or ice cream, or serve on its own.

SERVES 6

Sugar Cut-Out Cookies

This recipe makes dough that is easy to roll and cut, resilient, elastic, and yummy. The creative possibilities for this cookie at every holiday are nearly endless, and it is a wonderful family activity for any kind of day! Be sure to double this recipe if you want to have enough to share!

½ cup shortening or butter (or nondairy alternative)
1 cup granulated cane sugar
1 egg or egg substitute of choice (Like Egg Substitute # 1 or 2, page 15)
1 teaspoon vanilla extract, gluten-free
¼ cup milk (dairy or nondairy)
Food coloring (optional)
2¼ cups Jules Gluten Free All Purpose Flour (pages 6, 8)
2 teaspoons gluten-free baking powder
½ teaspoon salt
Sprinkles or colored sugar (optional)

▸ Cream shortening and sugar until very fluffy. Add egg, milk, vanilla extract, and food coloring, beating until integrated. Add the dry ingredients last, mixing until evenly blended. Form the dough into a ball and wrap tightly with plastic wrap. Refrigerate or freeze until cold and no longer sticky, at least 2 hours.

▸ Preheat the oven to 375°F (static) or 350°F (convection).

▸ Lightly flour the rolling surface, rolling pin, and cookie cutters with gluten-free flour. Roll the dough to approximately ⅛-inch thickness and cut shapes, rerolling dough to utilize all the dough.

▸ Place cut-out cookies onto a parchment-lined cookie sheet and decorate with colored sugar or sprinkles, if desired. Bake approximately 8–10 minutes until they begin to lightly brown at the edges. When baked and cooled, frost with Easy Cookie Icing, if desired.

MAKES 2 DOZEN COOKIES, DEPENDING ON SIZE

Easy Cookie Icing

1 cup sifted confectioners' sugar
¼ teaspoon vanilla extract, gluten-free
Milk (dairy or nondairy), as needed
Liquid food coloring (optional)

▸ Stir together sugar, vanilla, and milk, adding 1 tablespoon at time until a spreading consistency is achieved. Add food coloring, if desired.

▸ Store any leftover icing in a tightly sealed container in the refrigerator until the milk's expiration date.

MAKES 1 CUP ICING

Trifle with Summer Fruit

What a beautiful presentation of fresh fruits! And every bite is different. You'll be making this again and again, I guarantee it.

1 (3½-ounce) package instant vanilla pudding mix, gluten-free (some brands like Jell-O are currently dairy-free as well)

2 cups milk (dairy or nondairy)

5 large fresh peaches, peeled and sliced

1 tablespoon granulated cane sugar

1 pint strawberries, washed and sliced plus 4–5 additional unsliced strawberries for the top

½ cup blueberries, washed

1 Angel Food Cake (page 170) or use Eggless Cake recipe (page 204)

⅓ cup bourbon (or fruit juice)

1 cup whipped cream (dairy or nondairy)

Fresh mint sprigs

▸ Prepare the pudding mix according to the package directions, using the 2 cups of milk. Cover and chill for 5–10 minutes.

▸ Toss sliced peaches with granulated sugar and set aside in a separate bowl (if your peaches are not very ripe, start this step earlier and add more sugar). Wash and slice the strawberries and add to a bowl with the blueberries.

▸ Cut the prepared angel food cake into ½-inch cubes. Place half of these cake cubes on the bottom of a trifle dish or deep bowl; drizzle evenly with half the bourbon. Spoon half of the peaches over the cake, then add half of the berries. Pour half of the pudding over the peaches. Repeat the layers with the remaining ingredients, but reserve a few pieces of fruit for decorating the top of the cake. Cover with plastic wrap and chill for at least 2 hours.

▸ Spread the whipped cream over the top of the trifle just before serving and decorate with the mint sprigs.

SERVES 8–10

Tropical Pudding Cake

This cake is so moist with fruit that it is nearly a pudding, but it's still recognizably cake-like. Whatever naming quandary we have with this recipe, there is no mistaking how delicious it is!

CAKE:

¾ cup granulated cane sugar

½ cup butter or nondairy alternative

2 large eggs or egg substitute of choice (like Ener-G Egg Replacer or Egg Substitute #1 or 2, page 15)

3 bananas, very ripe and mashed

¼ cup unsweetened coconut milk

½ cup Jules Gluten Free All Purpose Flour (pages 6, 8)

1 teaspoon baking soda

¼ teaspoon sea salt

¼ cup pineapple, chopped and drained

½ cup shredded coconut (optional)

⅔ cup walnuts, chopped (optional; omit if making nut-free)

SAUCE:

1 teaspoon Jules Gluten Free All Purpose Flour (pages 6, 8)

1 cup plus 1 tablespoon unsweetened coconut milk

1 tablespoon granulated cane sugar

¼ teaspoon sea salt

continues

CAKE:

▸ Preheat the oven to 350°F (static) or 325°F (convection).

▸ Prepare a 9 x 9-inch square or a 9-inch round cake pan by spraying with cooking oil or buttering it.

▸ Cream sugar and butter until fluffy. Mix in eggs, bananas, and coconut milk. Gradually beat in the dry ingredients until incorporated. Stir in the pineapple and any optional ingredients at this point.

▸ Pour into a prepared pan and bake for approximately 50 minutes until lightly crisp around the edges and a cake tester inserted into the center of the cake comes out clean.

▸ Remove to cool slightly before serving.

SAUCE:

▸ In a small bowl, whisk the 1 teaspoon gluten-free flour into the 1 tablespoon coconut milk. Set aside to thicken.

▸ Heat the 1 cup of coconut milk gently in a small saucepan over medium temperature. As it is heating, stir in the sugar and salt, stirring until dissolved. Add in the flour/milk mixture and bring to a quick boil by raising the flame. Remove from the heat as soon as it boils and set it aside to cool. Pour the cooled sauce over the individual slices of cake before serving.

SERVES 4–6

INDEX